2D to VR with Unity5 and Google Cardboard

2D to VR with Unity5 and Google Cardboard

by
Roberto Dillon

CRC Press
Taylor & Francis Group
Boca Raton London New York

CRC Press is an imprint of the
Taylor & Francis Group, an **informa** business

AN A K PETERS BOOK

CRC Press
Taylor & Francis Group
6000 Broken Sound Parkway NW, Suite 300
Boca Raton, FL 33487-2742

Library of Congress Cataloging-in-Publication Data

Names: Dillon, Roberto, author.
Title: 2D to VR with Unity5 and Google Cardboard / Roberto Dillon.
Description: Boca Raton : Taylor & Francis, CRC Press, [2017]
Identifiers: LCCN 2016035592 | ISBN 9781498781527 (pbk. : alk. paper)
Subjects: LCSH: Computer games--Programming. | Unity (Electronic resource) |
Video games--Design. | Three-dimensional display systems. | Virtual
reality. | Google Cardboard (Three-dimensional display system)
Classification: LCC QA76.76.C672 D5338 2017 | DDC 794.8/1526--dc23
LC record available at https://lccn.loc.gov/2016035592

Visit the Taylor & Francis Web site at
http://www.taylorandfrancis.com

and the CRC Press Web site at
http://www.crcpress.com

Printed and bound in the United States of America by Sheridan

To Marina (1973–2007) and Davide (1973–2016)

Contents

Foreword

I WAS PROBABLY IN PRIMARY SCHOOL WHEN I STARTED dreaming about making games. In my head, games where made of ideas spawned from the imagination of the game designer, ideas that would be magically implemented in the software by the programming team. I wanted to be a game designer, and I thought programming was not something I had to dabble with.

Later on I found out that entering the game industry as a game designer was quite complicated because of the typical "Catch-22 dilemma:" nobody hires a designer without prior experience in the industry, but at the same time it's impossible to get industry experience without being in the industry in the first place. For somebody who couldn't afford to come out of a game design school, this was quite the problem.

My first foray into real game-making was using Adobe Flash around 2007. For the first time, Flash was allowing me to be the game designer, programmer, and even graphic artist, bridging the gap between my ideas and making them a reality that thousands of people could actually try.

The way games are made today is wildly different and this is true mostly thanks to the incredible pieces of software we have available. In time, game engines like Unity, Unreal Engine, Game Maker, Stencyl, Construct (and many others) had expanded on what Flash enabled in the first place, becoming a necessary tool to cope with the ever-changing landscape of platforms, consoles, technologies, and requirements. After Flash, in 2012 I chose Unity as my engine of choice for its flexibility and ease of use, and the huge community and amount of online resources and books available to learn.

I now work at Unity Technologies, and I am amazed every day by how fast the panorama changes and how quickly the company—and thus, the engine—reacts to it. New stores coming out everyday, new platforms, VR, rendering technologies, new controllers, new ways to monetize, a thousand different devices to support: being able to leave all these technical issues to the engine and focus on the gameplay is the biggest advantage we have over developers making games ten years ago.

With the power of these tools and several excellent didactical resources like the present book written by Roberto Dillon at your disposal, there's no excuse or strange industry Catch-22 to hold you off anymore. You have the potential to create something worthy, something inspiring, or—why not—the next masterpiece game.

Ciro Continisio
Technical Evangelist, Unity Technologies

Introduction

E VERY DAY SPENT IN THE WORLD OF GAME development seems more exciting than the previous one: new games, new technologies, and groundbreaking ideas seem to pop out of nowhere and amaze us in ways that were thought to be impossible not long ago. This technological revolution we live in was also made possible by the constant "democratization" of development that, thanks to state-of-the-art tools like the Unity game engine, has allowed many people to shape their ideas and create new and astonishing software with relative ease.

Unity itself is in constant evolution: new features are added by a very talented group of engineers, updates follow each other on a tight schedule, and plenty of good books covering different aspects of the engine are already available. Yet I felt there was still room for another volume that, like every good teacher should do, wouldn't try to teach "everything" that the engine offers today (including features that will doubtlessly become obsolete tomorrow), but would instead impart a thoughtful and sound knowledge enabling students to build a solid foundation upon which they will later be able to expand in the areas they are most interested in—whether mobile development, 2D games, or virtual reality (VR)—while staying up to date with the latest features.

To achieve this, the book is structured into four parts that integrate and complement each other to provide a comprehensive overview of what Unity has to offer. In the first part, after a general introduction, a simple 2D game prototype is explained in detail, giving us the opportunity to get used to several of the engine's fundamental building blocks, like scripting and Mecanim. Part II expands on the first by building a simple match-3 game to be deployed also on mobile, and Part III, instead, moves into 3D by building a first-person game that will also be experienced in VR through the wildly popular and inexpensive Google Cardboard.

The last part covers some additional topics that will help beginners in gaining a basic understanding of more advanced aspects of game development, like Physics and Shaders, besides offering an overview of the latest features added to Unity 5, like rewarded ads and in-app purchases, which are of fundamental importance to monetize modern mobile games. Example Unity packages based on the various chapters can be downloaded from the website http://ProgramAndPlay.com.

Finally, do note that, while this book is aimed at beginning Unity developers, a basic grasp of fundamental programming concepts, like variables, arrays, functions, classes, and so on, is assumed.

Enjoy your journey as a game developer with Unity: remember, we never stop learning, so be curious about anything that happens inside, as well as outside, the Unity community.

I really hope to play some of your own games soon!

Roberto Dillon
Singapore, July 14, 2016

Acknowledgments

SEVERAL PEOPLE HELPED ME during the writing of this book. I am especially grateful to Ciro Continisio and Tony Peters for their feedback and help, my students, the whole Unity community, and, of course, my family for their constant support. Special thanks, also, to Rick Adams and Jessica Vega from CRC Press/Taylor & Francis Group and Jennifer Brady from Deanta Global for turning this manuscript into a reality.

Author

Dr. Roberto Dillon is the author of several well-received game-related books published by AKPeters, CRC Press, and Springer, including *On the Way to Fun*, *The Golden Age of Video Games*, and *HTML5 Game Development from the Ground-Up with Construct 2*.

He is active both as an indie developer, through his Singapore-based studio, Adsumsoft, and as an academic in the field of game design and development. His games have been showcased at events like Sense of Wonder Night in Tokyo, FILE Games in Rio de Janeiro, and the Indie Prize Showcase at Casual Connect, besides reaching top positions on Apple's App Store and Google Play across several countries and categories.

He is currently an associate professor at James Cook University (JCU) in Townsville, Queensland, Australia, lecturing game design and project management classes. Before joining JCU, he was chair of the Game Software Design and Production Department at the DigiPen Institute of Technology, Singapore, teaching a variety of courses ranging from games history to game mechanics, with his students gaining top honors at competitions like the Independent Games Festival (IGF), both in San Francisco and Shanghai.

I

Our First Game

CHAPTER 1

Getting Around in Unity

FIRST RELEASED IN 2005, Unity is, today, one of the most powerful game engines on the market, besides being the most popular. It is a very flexible tool, which also means that it is actually a challenging program to master, but fear not: understanding its basic operation and starting to see the results of our hard work coming to life while also having fun is not that difficult, as we are going to see throughout this book.

Once we have downloaded and installed the latest version from Unity3d.com (remember to check all platforms you may be interested in, like Android, iOS, and so on, as shown in Figure 1.1), we are ready to launch the editor. In doing so, we will first be asked whether we want to load an existing project or start a new one. Let's opt for the latter and, like in Figure 1.2, decide on a name and a location where to save it.

Once in the main window, the layout will look like in Figure 1.3, and the first step we really need to work on is to familiarize ourselves with it.

Here, we can see a working layout split into different sections, each taking one or more tabs. Let's understand what its main features are.

The **Project** tab in the lower part of Figure 1.2 is dedicated to showing all the assets that our game will use. Here is where we will define directories to store any 3D model, sprite, or sound we need beside the actual level that will build the final game, called **Scenes**.

On top of it, there is a tab called **Hierarchy**. This will contain all the objects present in the current scene. As we see, by default, Unity adds a *main camera* and a *directional light*.

On its right, we have the actual *Scene* view (Figure 1.4).

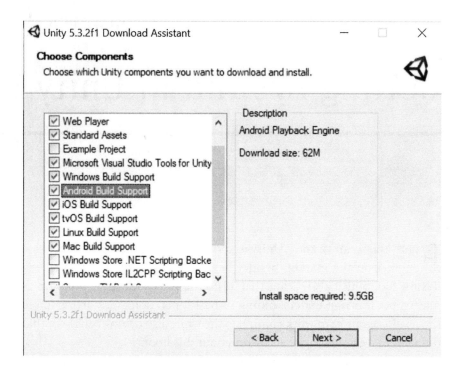

FIGURE 1.1   Installing Unity and its supporting files for different platforms.

FIGURE 1.2   Starting a new project. Notice the options to load any eventual asset package and to select a 3D or 2D starting mode. While our first project will be 2D, these settings can also be easily accessed and changed while working at a later time.

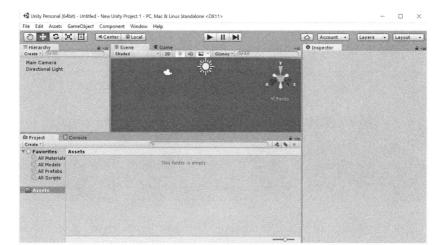

FIGURE 1.3   The default layout after starting an empty project.*

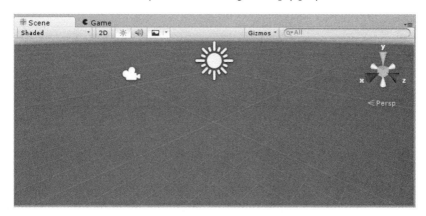

FIGURE 1.4   The Scene tab. We can use this to navigate throughout the level.

In Figure 1.3, notice the icons representing the objects in the *Hierarchy*: a camera and a light. On top of these, we can see another set of icons. These allow us to toggle some visual effects on/off, mute audio, switch lights, and switch between a 2D or 3D perspective (essentially, the same setting we could have altered when creating the project). Try the 2D icon to see how the perspective changes. Once back in 3D, we can also click the **Persp** label under the set of XYZ axes to switch to an isometric view of the scene. Clicking any of the axes will align the scene view to it.

---

* If your starting layout looks significantly different, select Layouts/Default from the Window menu.

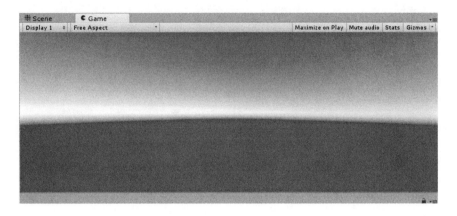

FIGURE 1.5   Selecting the Game tab shows the camera view. Here, we can choose to maximize the window when testing the game, mute the audio, and show some useful stats like frame rate, and so on.

We can also see a drop-down menu named **Gizmos**. These are additional icons allowing us to point out specific objects in a scene and can have various uses as visual debugging and setup aids. Anyway, we won't need them for the time being so, instead, let's click on the tab right next to *Scene*, labeled **Game**. This allows us to access the actual view of the camera (Figure 1.5).

Nothing much to look at here yet, since we have no actual objects. Unity adds a default skybox, though, so we can see a nice horizon line. Let's click back on the Scene tab and select the camera in the *Hierarchy* by clicking it. Clicking on an object will make all its properties, from its default current position and rotation values to customized components, appear in the last tab, the **Inspector** (Figure 1.6).

Navigating a scene and interacting with its object can be done by using the set of icons that are, by default, displayed on top of the *Hierarchy* tab (Figure 1.7)

In particular, selecting the *Hand* icon (which can also be done by using the key shortcut *Q*) allows us to freely move around the scene by keeping the left mouse button pressed, and rotating, by keeping the right mouse button pressed instead.

Pressing the *directional arrows* (shortcut *W*) will highlight a selected object with a set of axes (Figure 1.8), which we can then drag around to move the object itself (note that the object can also be moved freely in the 3D space by pressing the little cube next to the origin of the axis).

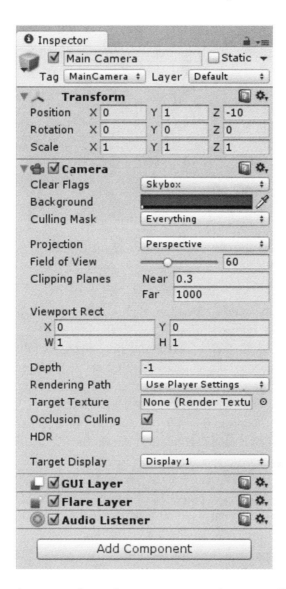

FIGURE 1.6   Selecting an object, the main camera in this case, will expose all its properties and components in the Inspector tab. Note the Transform component: this is a fundamental part of any object used to identify its position, rotation, and scaling factor.

FIGURE 1.7   A set of icons to move in the scene and manipulate selected objects (rotating, scaling, etc.).

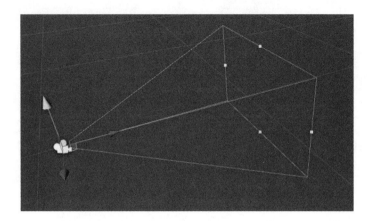

FIGURE 1.8   Selecting the main camera and the Directional Arrows icon will allow us to move it around the 3D space by interacting with the set of axes popping out over the object itself.

Try moving the camera around and see how its *Transform* values in the *Inspector* tab change accordingly.

The next two icons (shortcuts *E* and *R*, respectively) allow us to rotate and scale the selected object following the very same approach, while the last one (shortcut *T*) allows us to interact and resize graphical user interface (GUI) elements, as we will see in later chapters.

Let's try now to add an object to our scene, for example, a cube. As shown in Figure 1.9, click on the *Create* menu within the *Hierarchy* tab and select the *3D Object/Cube* option. If necessary, move it around so that it falls into the visual field of the camera, and we can see it in the *Game* tab. A useful tip here: if you lose sight of an object, like the cube in this case, you can quickly center the scene view on it by double clicking on it in the *Hierarchy* or selecting it in the *Hierarchy* first, moving back the mouse cursor on the *Scene* tab, and then pressing the key *F* (for "focus").

We may also add another icon to it, a "Gizmo" like those we briefly introduced earlier, which may be useful to label the object within the editor. To do this, click on the colored cube next to the object's name in the Inspector (Figure 1.10).

Unity's interface can actually showcase many more tabs than those introduced here, and we will see several more, starting from the next chapter. These are accessible via the *Window* menu and offer us plenty of information on the current game: we can have tabs showing a console window (fundamental for quick debugging), an audio mixer, animation, lighting, and so on. A very particular window we can open is the **Asset**

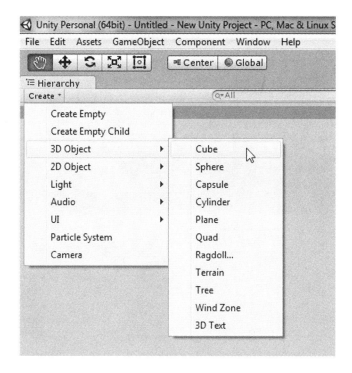

FIGURE 1.9   Adding a cube to the scene.

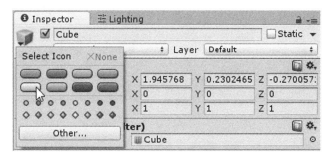

FIGURE 1.10   Adding an icon to objects may be a good idea to keep track of things if the editor starts getting too crowded. We can add labels or simple dots/diamonds, or even use our own textures.

Store, where we can access lots of free and paid resources for our Unity games (Figure 1.11).

Before concluding this introductory chapter, one more, very important feature of Unity's interface and layout to note is that it is actually highly customizable: every tab and window we saw so far can actually be dragged around and placed anywhere in the screen, allowing us to configure

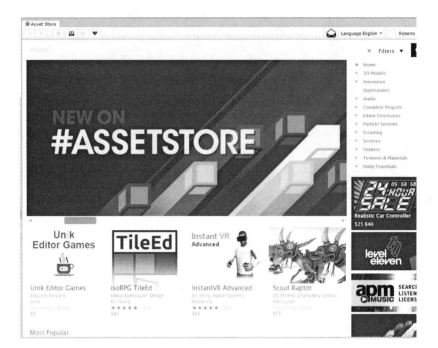

FIGURE 1.11   Unity Asset Store. We can buy assets and import them directly into our project from here.

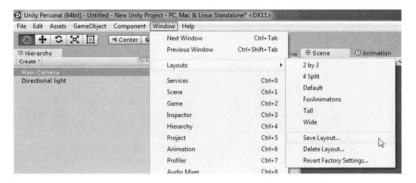

FIGURE 1.12   We can configure Unity's layout according to several presets, as well as make our own custom ones that we can save and reload any time.

a customized layout that fits our working style and preferences. A few default setups are accessible via a dedicated menu (Figure 1.12), through which we can also save our own.

Try a few different ones, and try moving some tabs around as well; don't worry, you can always go back by picking the Default menu item if things get out of control!

Note: Throughout the development of the games included in the book, I will use a Windows-based PC. The Unity Mac version has no significant differences, though, with the exception that the latter has a *Unity* menu that includes a few items that are split across the *Edit* (like Preferences and Modules) and *Help* (About, Manage License) menus on the PC. Besides, key shortcuts involve the "Command" key instead of the CTRL key.

CHAPTER 2

Setting Up a Platform Game

Having acquired a basic understanding of the Unity working environment, we can now proceed in our exploration and study. In this chapter, we will begin a simple platform game prototype, featuring a running and jumping player-controlled sprite, an enemy, objects to pick, and so on. It is a very simple project, but it will allow us to introduce several fundamental concepts and get us acquainted with actual game development in Unity.

First of all, let's start a new project and set default settings to 2D as in Figure 2.1.

We will be presented with the familiar Unity layout. Let's leave the Main Camera setting to its default values (of particular importance here is the "Size" parameter, as this will determine the actual span of the viewport; and be sure that projection stays to "Orthographic" to keep the 2D perspective) and start by setting up a proper directory structure, including folders for "Animations," "Graphics," "Prefabs," "Sounds," and "Scripts" (naturally, we can add more any time as the need arises, but it's generally a good idea to keep things neat from the very beginning). Save the current scene (named "game" in this example), and we will have something like Figure 2.2 now. Note that, by default, the scene will be saved in the Project Root folder.

For this example, we are going to use the art assets available at http://opengameart.org/content/minimal-sidescroller-tileset.

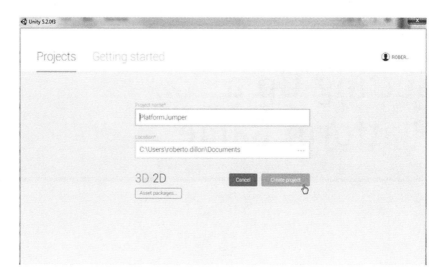

FIGURE 2.1   Starting a new project. Remember to set the project location to your own usual working directory!

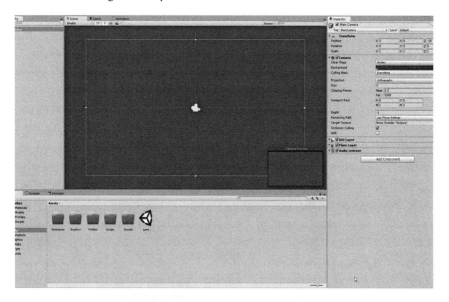

FIGURE 2.2   The Unity layout for this project. Note the white rectangle in the scene view outlining the camera viewport.

Download all of them, and then let's start by dragging and dropping the file "background_32.png" into our Graphics folder. As we see in Figure 2.3, the file will be automatically recognized as a texture and imported as a sprite.

FIGURE 2.3   Importing an image into the project.

Before proceeding any further, we should first have a look at the sprite properties and clarify any possible confusion; in particular, we should take a couple of minutes to fully understand the meaning of "pixels per unit" and its implications.

Having a sprite set to "100 pixels per unit," like the default value in our texture, simply means that 100 pixels would equal 1 unit in the game scene. In general, most developers assume 1 unit in the game world to equal 1 m, and build their game accordingly, but that is arbitrary. What is important, here, is that we remain consistent with our decision and scale all the various objects accordingly.

For smaller objects, like sprites or tiles sized 16 × 16 pixels, setting "pixels per unit" to their original dimension (i.e., 16, in this case) may actually be a handy choice, as it will help in aligning and snapping them together in the game layout, since they would fill exactly 1 in-game unit.

Note, also, that objects' size may affect performance if using Physics, as bigger objects (i.e., less pixels per unit) will require more computational power, since the engine may be moving something as big as hundreds of in-game units in each frame.

We may also wonder what "mipmaps" are. These are progressively smaller versions of the original texture that can be used when the object is far away from the camera to improve performance. This comes at a memory cost, though, as storing mipmaps will require a 33 percent increase in memory usage. For our small example, whether mipmaps are generated or not doesn't really matter but, in general, the suggestion is to always use mipmaps for all textures except for those used in the graphical user interface (GUI), since these will always be in front of the camera and will never be minified.

Enough theory for now. Let's get back to Unity and create a new Sprite object by right-clicking on the Hierarchy tab, Create Menu, as shown in Figure 2.4.

We can rename this sprite "background," associate the "background_32" texture to it by clicking on the Sprite field in the Object Renderer component (Figure 2.5), and then scale the sprite to cover the whole camera viewport (by selecting the Scaling tool, Figure 2.6).

Now, we want to add a few platforms on top of the background image. To do so, let's drag and drop the file "tileset_32_0.png" into the Graphics folder. This is a sprite sheet, so, in the Inspector, we need to select for "Multiple Sprites" (Figure 2.7) and then click on "Sprite Editor," where we need to select the Slice option (Figure 2.8).

Once back in the main Unity window, we can see (Figure 2.9) in the Project panel that the sprite sheet has been automatically divided into all its individual images!

Following the same steps we did earlier for the "Background" object, let's create a new Sprite object, name it **Platform**, and then pick the bridge-like sprite from the tileset (Figure 2.10).

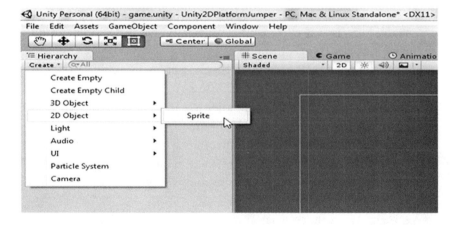

FIGURE 2.4   Adding a new sprite into the scene.

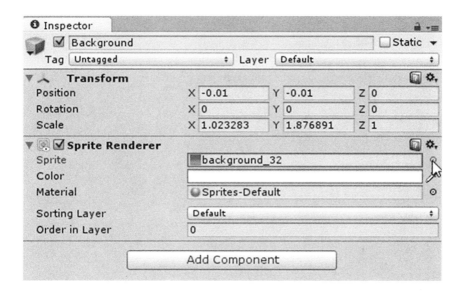

FIGURE 2.5   Choosing the previously imported image as the sprite of the newly created object.

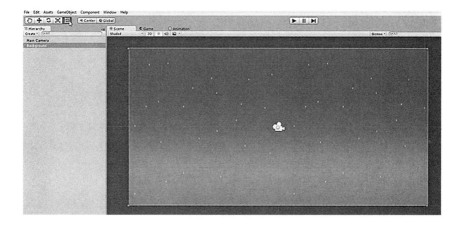

FIGURE 2.6   Selecting the resizing tool and then enlarging the Background object to fill up the camera viewport.

We can then resize and place "Platform" in the lower left part of the game area (Figure 2.11). It is now also a good time to turn this object into a *prefab*, a sort of template we can use to instantiate other objects sharing all the properties and characteristics of the original object. To do so, simply drag and drop "Platform" into the Assets/Prefabs folder in the Project tab. Note how the original object has now turned blue, from the original black,

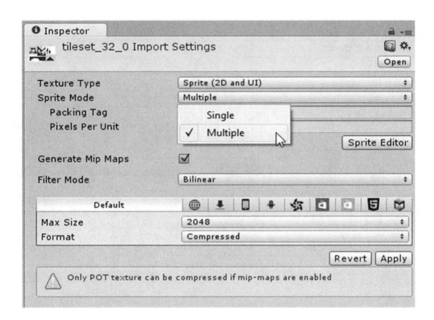

FIGURE 2.7   Importing a sprite sheet: Sprite Mode property has to be set to "Multiple."

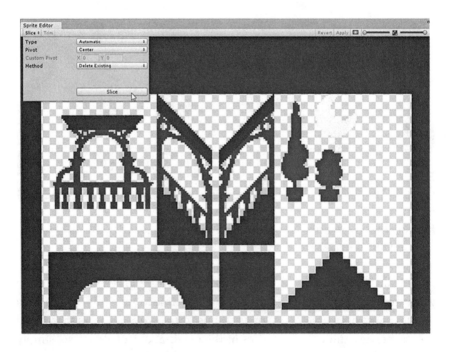

FIGURE 2.8   Unity's built-in Sprite Editor. Here, we can extract individual sprites from the imported sheet.

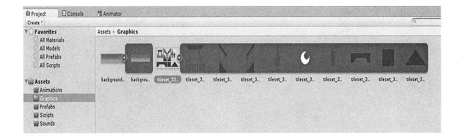

FIGURE 2.9   The sprite sheet after subdividing into individual sprites.

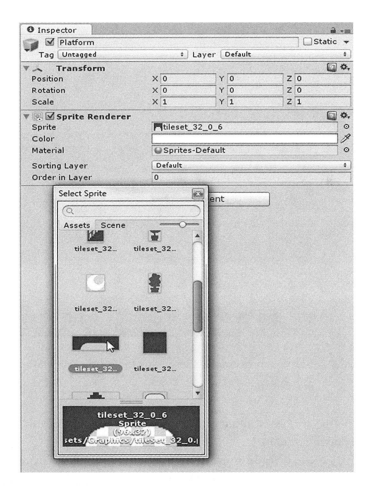

FIGURE 2.10   Selecting the bridge image for the newly defined Platform sprite.

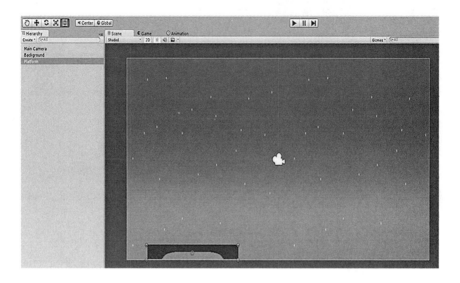

FIGURE 2.11   Placing the sprite in the scene.

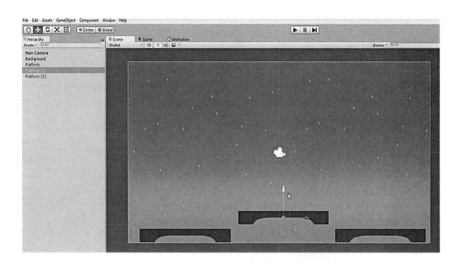

FIGURE 2.12   Adding more bridges after having turned the original sprite into a prefab.

to signify that it is not a stand-alone object any more but is now derived from an existing prefab.

We can now easily add some more platforms to the level by dragging the prefab back into the scene, and then arrange them, after selecting the Moving tool right below the Edit menu (Figure 2.12).

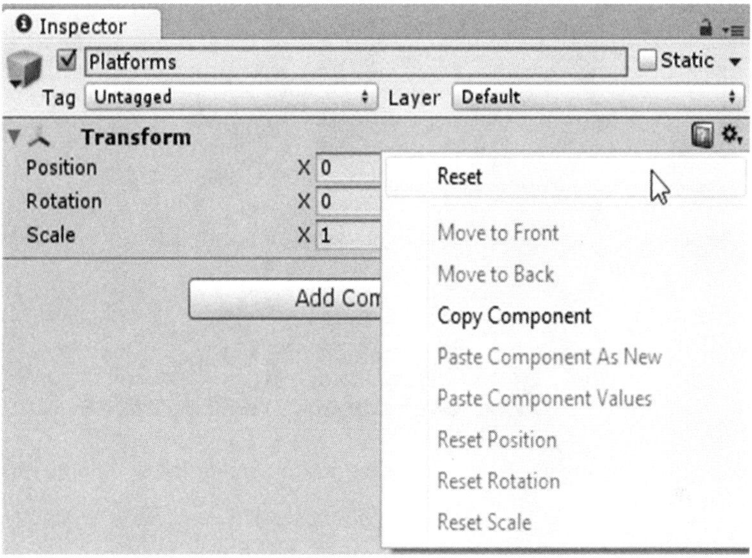

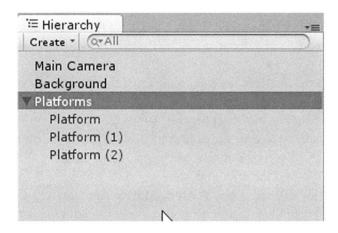

FIGURE 2.13   For each component, its settings can be reset via the small cog in the upper right corner of the component itself in the Inspector tab.

FIGURE 2.14   Nesting objects. This will make handling objects of the same type much easier, besides keeping the Hierarchy tab neat and tidy.

To keep things neat, let's group all the platforms together: create a new empty object, name it "Platforms," and be sure that its origin is set to (0,0,0) so that it is centered in the game world origin (if not, click on its Settings cog as shown in Figure 2.13). Then, bring all the other platform objects into this one, effectively turning the former into "children" of the latter (Figure 2.14).

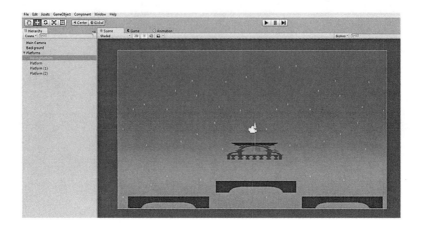

FIGURE 2.15   Placing a different platform on the screen. We will make this one move left and right.

Let's try to add a moving platform now.

Start by creating a new Sprite object (again, by explicitly creating one in the Hierarchy or by simply dragging and dropping an image you like from the sprite sheet in the Graphics folder into the Hierarchy). Let's resize it and place it roughly in the middle of the screen like in Figure 2.15. Last, make a prefab out of it as well; maybe we will add more of them in future!

To move the platform, we can proceed in different ways: we could write a script to do so programmatically, or we could use Unity's *Mecanim* animation system. For learning purposes, let's do ... both!

It is actually high time for us to start delving into the scripting side of things, so let's begin by coding a very simple script in C#.

Select **MovingPlatform** and click on *Add Component, New Script* (Figure 2.16). Call the script **PlatformMoveScript*** and click on **Create and Add** to actually add it to the project and as an additional component to the current, selected object. Once done, move the script from the Asset folder (where it gets placed by default) into our Scripts folder to keep the project tidy.

Once done, open it by double clicking on the Script icon. This will open either MonoDevelop or Visual Studio, according to your preferences and the version of Unity you have installed. Note that, while Unity on PC can

---

* Feel free to label the scripts in any way you like. The only thing to remember is that the script name and the name of the class being defined there have to be the same.

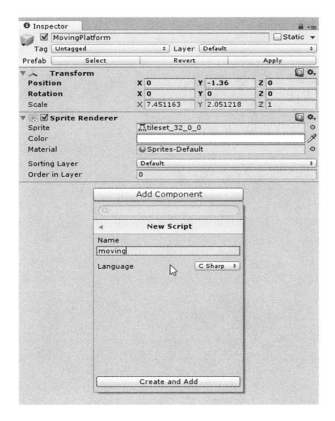

FIGURE 2.16   Adding a new script to an existing object. That's how we can actually control and interact with objects in the scene during the game.

use both, the Mac version comes only with MonoDevelop. In any case, on PC, the default script editor can be changed any time via the menu item **Edit/Preferences** and then by selecting the **External Tools** section.*

Once the script opens in our editor of choice, it will show a default script skeleton like in Figure 2.17.

In our script (fully shown later), we need, first, to define a couple of public variables to store the actual platform speed and where we want it to change direction. Both are defined as float, and, as public variables, we can easily access them via other scripts/objects or even at runtime via the Inspector tab, for testing purposes.

---

* Visual Studio is an extremely powerful and flexible integrated development environment (IDE), but MonoDevelop is somewhat easier to understand and use, so I would recommend the latter to beginners.

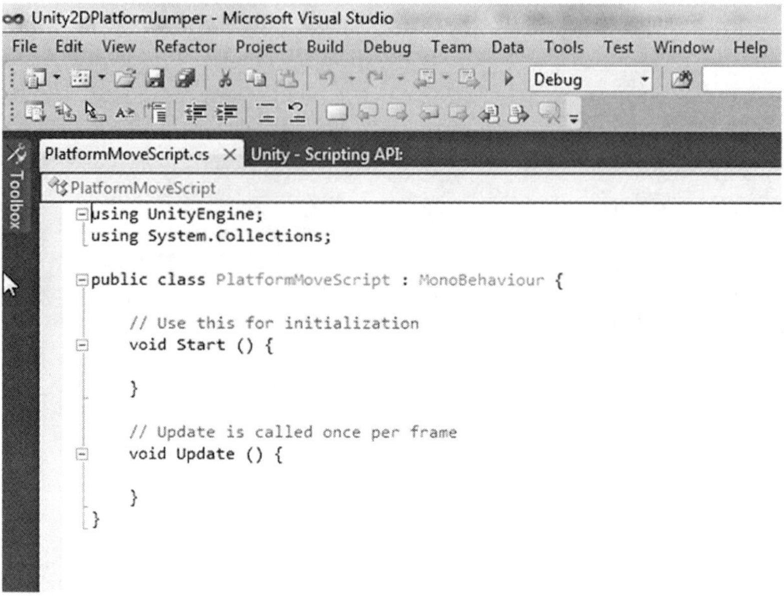

FIGURE 2.17 Every script starts with a *Start* and an *Update* method. Every instruction in the former will be executed when the script is first called, while anything in the latter will be executed in every frame.

All our coding will happen in the Update function. Here, we first declare a local variable of type float to store the current position of the platform, which is retrieved by accessing the Transform component and then its position along the *x* axis. Note that the "this" keyword before "transform" is not explicitly required, as it is automatically assumed by Unity to be there, but I personally like adding it anyway, as it may help in keeping more complex scripts, where we have to access different objects, readable. Then, before moving, we check whether we reached the predefined boundary position and, if affirmative, we change direction. We also multiply the speed value for "Time.deltaTime." This is the time lapsed in between frames and is used to keep movement frame independent.

```
using UnityEngine;
using System.Collections;

public class PlatformMoveScript : MonoBehaviour {

    // public variables are exposed in the Inspector and
can easily be changed at runtime and be accessed by
other components or objects.
```

```
public float speed = 2f;
public float boundary = 7f;
// Use this for initialization
   void Start () {
   }
   // Update is called once per frame
   void Update () {
      // declaring a variable to store current
position.
      // Using "this" is not required but can make
things more comprehensible in complex scripts.
   float x = this.transform.position.x;
   // once we reach a certain position, we change
direction. Otherwise, keep moving
   if (x > boundary)   {
        speed *= -1;
        // necessary as platform may go beyond 7 and
then remain stuck there as direction changes every
frame.
        this.transform.position.Set(boundary,0f,0f);
   }
   else if (x < -boundary) {
        speed *= -1;
        this.transform.position.Set(-boundary, 0f, 0f);
   }
   this.transform.Translate(speed * Time.deltaTime,
0f, 0f);
      }
}
```

Save the script and then, with the *MovingPlatform* object selected, check the Inspector to see the public variables we discussed earlier ready to be modified (Figure 2.18).

Start the game to test if everything we did so far works: you should now see the platform moving back and forth (Figure 2.19)!

Now is a good time to have a quick introduction to debugging. Once we start coding, sooner or later we will realize that things don't go as expected: errors may be reported by Unity in the Console window, and programs won't start at all or, if they do, there may be some unexpected behaviors that we need to fix. Very common mistakes include forgetting to close a bracket or missing a semicolon; these errors can actually

FIGURE 2.18 The script showing up now in the Inspector. Public variables can be accessed and changed from here.

FIGURE 2.19 Our current platformer: not much to show yet, but the top platform is moving back and forth according to the speed and boundaries set in our script.

be caught quickly, even before going back into Unity to test the game: in MonoDevelop, for example, we can already build the project via the *Build* menu (shortcuts *F8* on Windows, *Command + B* on OSX), and any syntax error will be highlighted for us right away. On the other hand, when the game does start, and things work in unexpected ways, the real trouble begins. Diving into portions of code to find what's wrong is an art in its own right, and any professional-level IDE, like MonoDevelop and Visual Studio, does offer different advanced tools to help. While those are beyond the scope of this book, Unity does provide us with some simple instructions that are suitable for beginners, which can make our lives much easier in tracing back variables and the overall program flow.

The most important instruction at our disposal is *print()* (or its longer form *Debug.log()*). It can be added anywhere in our code, and what it does is print out a specified message in the Console tab. You may have noticed this already: by default, it is placed next to the Project tab, and all errors and warning messages will be displayed there. So, if, for example, in our previous script we want to know exactly when the moving platform reaches the boundary and turns back, we could simply add the following line right before multiplying *speed* by −1:

```
print ("Turning around now!");
```

Note, also, that we can concatenate text and variables in the same print statement like this:

```
print ("Variable X now is:" + X);
```

In the end, print() is an extremely useful method that we will likely use a lot to check whether a method is actually being called and to track changes to variables that don't seem to behave as expected, so that we can figure out where the problems actually are.

Now, let's go back to our moving platform and try to achieve the same results without code, using Mecanim instead. Deselect the script in the Inspector to deactivate it (or you can remove it altogether if you prefer), as shown in Figure 2.20.

To add animations to any object, we need, first, to add the "Animator" component to the object itself (Figure 2.21; after clicking the "Add Component" button, we find it in the "Miscellaneous" group).

To work, the Animator needs a "Controller," which, in turn, will be responsible for handling the various animations and their respective transitions.

It is a good idea now to bring up both the "Animation" and "Animator" windows and dock them, as in Figure 2.22. After selecting the object we want to animate, that is, **MovingPlatform** in our case, we can now easily create a new animation with an associated controller by simply clicking on the "Create" button displayed in the middle of the Animation window (otherwise,

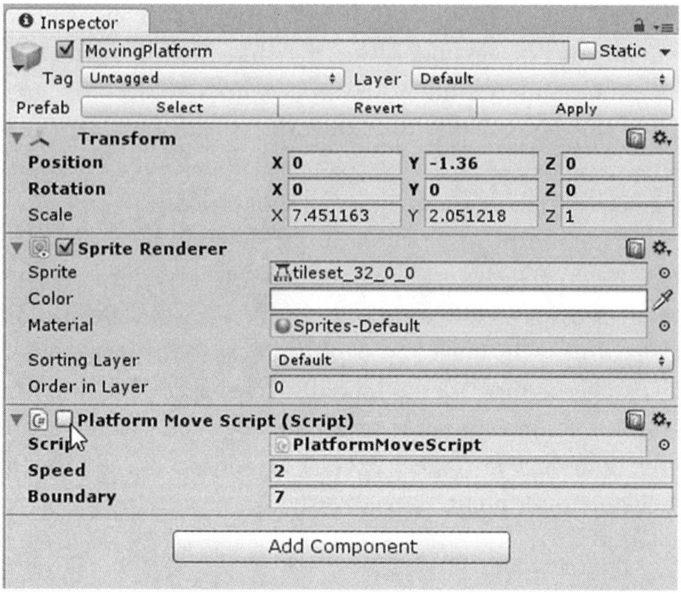

FIGURE 2.20 Clicking on the checkbox next to the component's name deselects it. If we run the game now, the platform won't move anymore, since the script responsible for it has been deselected.

we can create everything by using the usual "Create" menu in the Project tab). These will be automatically placed in our Animation project folder, and the controller will already be selected in our object's Animator component.

In our case, we want to "animate" the position of the object, so, by clicking the **Add Property** button, we shall look for the **Transform—Position** property and add it (Figure 2.23).

We will now be presented with a time line where we can add *keyframes* specifying the value that our selected property needs to have at that given instant. Unity will take care of interpolating the value across the keyframes for us and will record any change we make to the variables, as long as the little red dot button on the top left corner of the Animation tab is pressed/highlighted.

In our case, we may want to have the platform move to the far right in 2 seconds, then go to the far left after another 4 seconds, and then back to the center in another 2 seconds, ready for the animation to loop. This can be achieved as shown in Figure 2.24.

Since we didn't define any further states (i.e., animations) in the controller besides **leftright**, nor any additional transition, the animation is automatically set to loop (Figure 2.25).

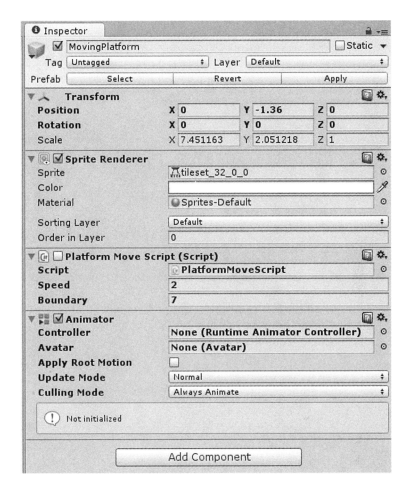

FIGURE 2.21 The MovingPlatform object after having added the "Animator" component. We need a "Controller" to act like a "Finite State Machine" (FSM)* and handle any animation and corresponding transitions.

Note also that Unity doesn't simply interpolate linearly across values but does so following different curves, generating some nice transition effects, as we can appreciate by clicking on the Curves tab within the Animation window (Figure 2.26).

Testing the game now will show the platform moving across the screen following the sinusoidal movement as defined previously (Figure 2.27).

---

* FSMs are very simple but powerful constructs used in computer science to model different types of behaviors. They are made by a set of predefined states (like "Run" or "Hide") and conditions to trigger the shift between them (like "Being Chased" or "Being Discovered"). An introduction to the topic can be found here: http://bit.ly/1WNjaW4.

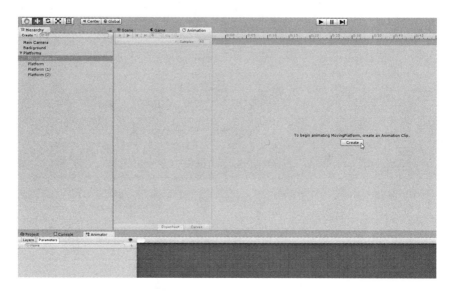

FIGURE 2.22   With the "MovingPlatform" object selected and the Animation and Animator windows ready and docked in the layout, we are ready to create a new animation and its required controller.

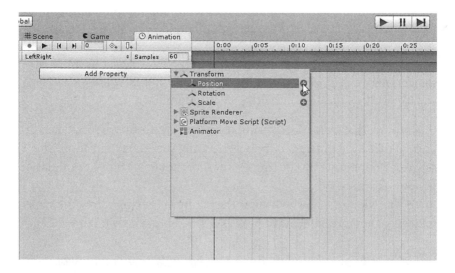

FIGURE 2.23   Adding the Position property, that is, what we want to control in our animation.

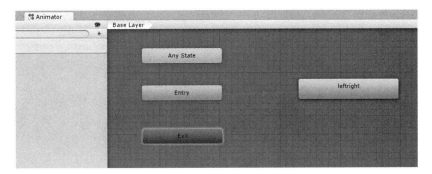

FIGURE 2.24   Setting up the animation. Scroll with the mouse wheel to zoom in/out of the time line. Click on the time line to move the current frame (i.e., move the red vertical line), and click on the little square + to add a keyframe there. With the keyframe selected, modify the *x* variable as required.

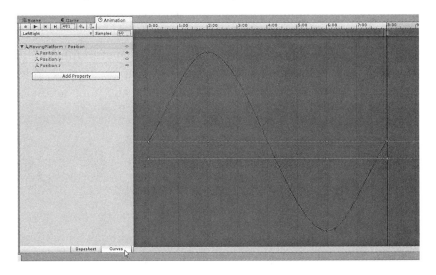

FIGURE 2.25   The Animator tab, showing our new animation, "leftright," which is automatically linked to the default "Entry" state.

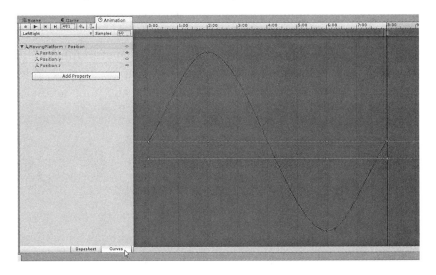

FIGURE 2.26   As we see from the graph, while the *y* and *z* positions remain fixed, the *x* coordinate changes following a sine curve.

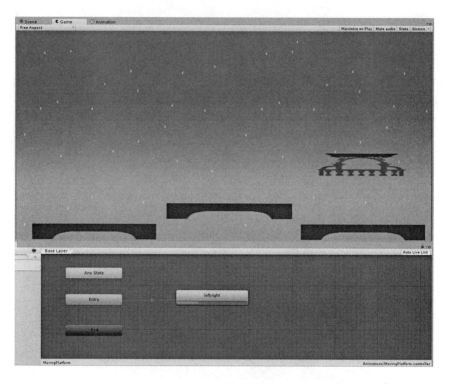

FIGURE 2.27 The running game, the top platform moves following the key-frames we defined in the *Animation* window, while the *Animator* window in the lower part of the screen monitors the current position within the animation time line (the blue progress bar at the bottom of the **leftright** animation state).

Feel free to take a short break now, and be sure that everything we did so far is crystal clear, then proceed to the next chapter: it's time to add a playable character to our game and make it run and jump across the platforms!

CHAPTER 3

Running and Jumping

For our playing hero, head back to *OpenGameArt.org* and pick a simple 2D animated sprite like the cat fighter that we can download from http://opengameart.org/content/cat-fighter-sprite-sheet. Unzip the file and drag *cat_fighter_sprite1.png* (Figure 3.1) into our Graphics project folder. Be sure it is imported as a **Sprite (2D and GUI)**, set its **Sprite Mode** to **Multiple**, **Pixels Per Unit** to 25 (otherwise the cat may look too small compared to the resized platforms), and open it in the editor to slice it like we did for the other sprite sheet in the previous chapter.

We can now create a new 2D object of type sprite and call it **Player** in the Hierarchy. Associate one of the individual cat sprites to the Sprite field in the Sprite Renderer component so that we can actually see the player in the game, and place it next to the platform in the lower left corner of the screen (Figure 3.2).

Let's now add an *Animator* component to the Player object and then create an Animator *Controller* called, for example, **PlayerCtr** in the project Animations folder. Make this the controller for the player in the Inspector (Figure 3.3).

With the Player object selected, open the Animator and Animations tabs: the former will have its default "Entry," "Exit," and "Any State," while the latter is ready for us to start adding some animations. In particular, we are now going to define an *Idle*, a *Walking*, and a *Jumping* animation by using the cat frames.

Let's start with **PlayerIdle**: as soon as we create a new animation, a corresponding state is also added to the Animator tab and linked to the "Entry" state as shown in Figure 3.4.

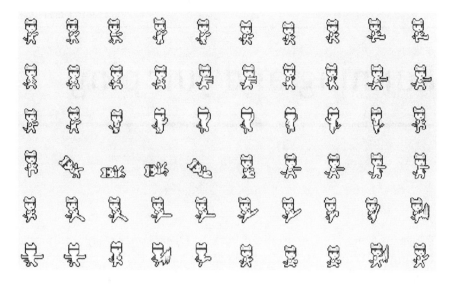

FIGURE 3.1 A sprite sheet with a simple character (downloaded from OpenGameArt.org) and animations we could use in our 2D platform games.

FIGURE 3.2 Placing the playable character in the scene.

Pick a few frames from those available in the cat fighter sprite sheet and drag them into the animation time line. Notice how a keyframe is added for each sprite we drop into the time line. In the end, we should have something like in Figure 3.5.

If we play the game now, the Player sprite will actually enter with the idle state and animate accordingly!

Let's now create a new animation clip (Figure 3.6) and call it **PlayerRun**. Select the frames to make up the animation (Figure 3.7). The animation

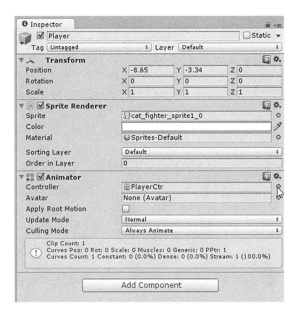

FIGURE 3.3   Making PlayerCtr the controller for the player's Animator.

FIGURE 3.4   Adding a new animation, named "PlayerIdle."

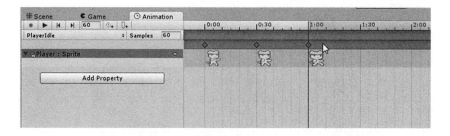

FIGURE 3.5   The actual "PlayerIdle" animation.

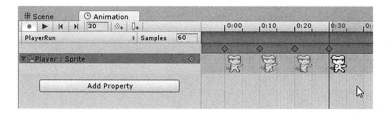

FIGURE 3.6   Creating a new clip.

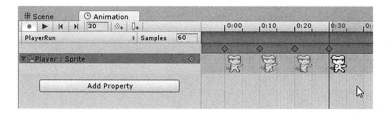

FIGURE 3.7   The "PlayerRun" animation, using frames 0, 3, 4, and 5 from the original sprite sheet.

can be tested right away by pressing the "Play" button (note that you may have to undock the "Game" tab as shown in Figure 3.8 if you want to see the animation's frame-by-frame progress in the Animation tab as well as the actual game).

With two animations in place, it is now time to arrange for a proper transition.

First of all, in the Animator window, let's right click on "PlayerIdle" and select **Make Transition** (Figure 3.9). This will allow us to draw an arrow to any other available state. In this case, let's connect "PlayerIdle" with "PlayerRun."

Then, still in the Animator tab, we have to add a parameter of type float. Call it **speed**. This will be the trigger between the two states, run and idle (Figure 3.10).

FIGURE 3.8   Testing the "PlayerRun" animation. The Game tab is now undocked and shown in its own independent window, so that we can check it against the Animation tab.

FIGURE 3.9   Making a transition between states.

Clicking on the transition itself will show its properties in the Inspector. Here, we can fine-tune how the transition works: in our case, we want it to be fast, so that the controls will feel tight and snappy. To achieve this, we should move the cursors defining the entrance and exit between the states accordingly. By clicking on the + sign in the **Conditions** section, we can then associate the **speed** variable to the transition and make it responsible for triggering the move between the two states (Figure 3.11).

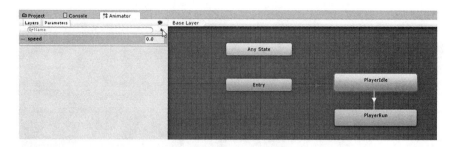

FIGURE 3.10   Once the transition is set between states, we have to decide how to trigger it. Here, we will be using the "speed" variable.

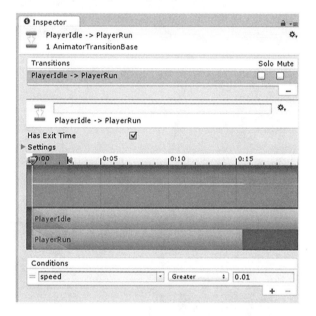

FIGURE 3.11   The transition between idle and run will happen when "speed" has a value greater than 0.01, meaning the player is actually moving the sprite around. Note that, if we want the transition to happen instantly, we need to uncheck the "Has Exit Time" flag. With this checked, instead, we can finely control the time required for transitioning between the two states.

When "speed" gets less than the previously defined threshold of 0.1, we should also go back from the run state to the idle one. As a simple exercise, create a new transition that accomplishes this.

By following the same steps, we should also add a new state for jumping, called **PlayerJump**, and a corresponding animation (this can be a very simple one, possibly using only "cat_fighter_sprite1_30" as a single frame). The new state needs to have transitions to and from both **PlayerIdle** and **PlayerRun**,

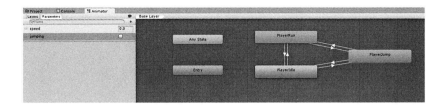

FIGURE 3.12 The Animator component for the Player object after having added a "jumping" parameter of type bool, the PlayerJump state, and corresponding transitions.

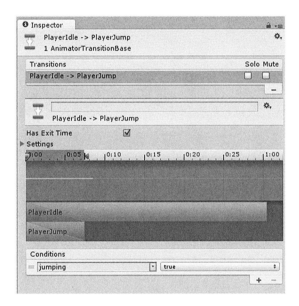

FIGURE 3.13 Transition from idle to jump states, triggered when "jumping" becomes true. Transitioning between run and jump states works in the same way.

and the transition should happen thanks to a new parameter of type bool defined within the Animator component. We can call this **jumping**; when true, it will trigger the transition to the jumping state and, when false, force us to go back to either idle or running states, according to the value of the other parameter, "speed." All these steps are shown in Figures 3.12 through 3.14.

If we test the game now (Figure 3.15), we can change the value of "speed" and "jumping" in the Animator window and see the different animations play in the Game window.

Our cat doesn't move yet by direct input from the player, though, and there are a few more steps we need to take care of before we can have a fully playable character.

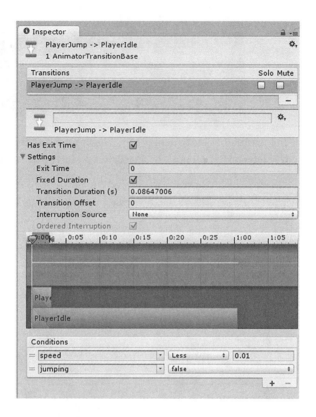

FIGURE 3.14   For transitioning back from jump to either idle or run, we need to check, besides that "jumping" is false, also the "speed" parameter.

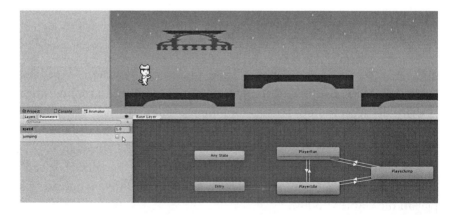

FIGURE 3.15   We can change states and check that all transitions work fine while in-game by modifying the "speed" and "jumping" variables in the Animator tab. Our cat will react accordingly.

To achieve this, we need to start working with Unity's built-in 2D Physics support, which will also help us in checking for collision detection.

First off, let's add a **Rigidbody 2D** component to *Player* (we find it under the Physics2D section after clicking on "Add Component" in the Inspector with Player selected). Then add a **Box Collider 2D** component as well.

Selecting the player in the scene will now show a thin green bounding box around him: that's what the Physics engine will look at to check for collisions with other objects (Figure 3.16).

Once this is done, if we start the game, we will see our poor cat fall helplessly down the screen! How come? Simple—gravity and physics are working fine, but our platforms are just a sprite, since we haven't added a *collider* to them for checking collisions with other objects yet!

Let's fix this right away: select the Platform prefab, so that any change we make will automatically be applied to all existing instances of the object, and add the **Box Collider 2D** component. Since we are adding colliders, let's add one to the MovingPlatform prefab as well. We may want to change its scale and offset values, too, so that the collider is aligned only with the upper part of the platform (Figure 3.17).

Starting the game again will have the cat now land on the platform and stay there, idle, as expected.

So, how do we move the cat? Let's add a new C# script component to the Player object and simply call it **PlayerScript** (this will, by default, be saved in the Asset folder. Don't forget to manually move it in the proper Scripts folder that we created earlier).

Open and edit the script as follows:

```
using UnityEngine;
using System.Collections;

public class PlayerScript : MonoBehaviour {

    // these variables are publicly exposed and can be
changed by other objects
    public float speed = 2f;
    public float jumpPower = 7f;

    // rigidbody and animator components need to be
accessed by declaring a variable of their
corresponding type first.
```

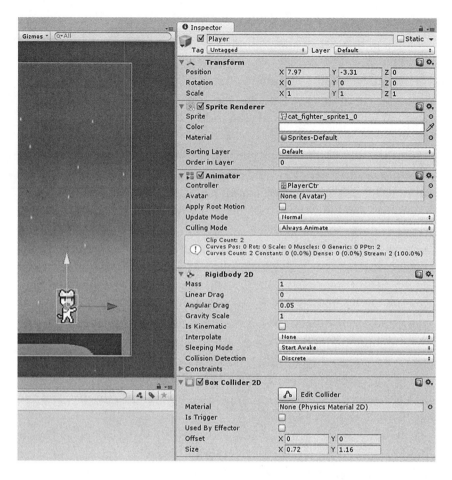

FIGURE 3.16 The Player sprite with its Inspector properties, showing the Rigidbody 2D and Box Collider 2D components. The size of the collider can be easily modified right from the Inspector window if needed.

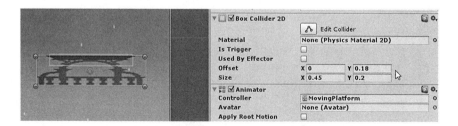

FIGURE 3.17 Editing the collider for the moving platform so that it matches the shape of the sprite.

```
  private Rigidbody2D rb2d;
  private Animator pAnim;
  // Use this for initialization
  void Start() {
    // retrieve the components
    rb2d = gameObject.GetComponent<Rigidbody2D>();
    pAnim = gameObject.GetComponent<Animator>();
  }
  void FixedUpdate() {
    // handles horizontal movement
    float h = speed * Input.GetAxisRaw("Horizontal")
* Time.deltaTime;
    // the gravity force will pull the cat down
    float v = jumpPower * Input.GetAxisRaw("Vertical")
* Time.deltaTime;

    if (Mathf.Abs(v) > 0.01)
      pAnim.SetBool("jumping", true);
    else
      pAnim.SetBool("jumping", false);

    pAnim.SetFloat("speed", Mathf.Abs(h));

    // to mirror the animation, we flip the scale x
value when running left:
    if (Input.GetAxisRaw("Horizontal") == -1 && this.
transform.localScale.x == 1)
    {
      this.transform.localScale = new Vector3(-1f,
1f, 1f);
    }
    if (Input.GetAxisRaw("Horizontal") == 1 && this.
transform.localScale.x == -1)
    {
      this.transform.localScale = new Vector3(1f, 1f,
1f);
    }
    // move according to input!
    rb2d.transform.Translate(h * this.transform.
localScale.x, v, 0f);
  }
}
```

Let's now discuss this code in detail, to understand what we have done and how it works.

First of all, we declare two public variables, *speed* and *jumpPower*: these determine how fast and how high we can jump, and, by making them public, we can easily change them at runtime to fine-tune their values as well as access them from different objects if the need arises. Then, we declare two other private variables of *Rigidbody 2D* and Animator types. This is a necessary step in Unity5 to later access such components within the object itself, something we do right away in the *Start()* function. This method is called on in the creation of the object that the script is attached to.

Once we have set the references to the player's rigid body and animator, we are ready to proceed. Note that here we are writing code in the *FixedUpdate()* function instead of the more common *Update()* method, which is automatically set up by Unity in the default script skeleton. The reason is that Update() is called every frame and, as such, time between calls is inconsistent because frame rate can fluctuate during execution. Any object using Physics (i.e., having a Rigidbody component attached to it) should, instead, be updated at a consistent interval, which is exactly what FixedUpdate() does, being called regularly by the Physics engine.

Then, in FixedUpdate(), we start by declaring two local variables of type float. These will store the current values for horizontal (h) and vertical (v) movement, which are obtained by multiplying either **speed** or **jumpPower**, for **Input.GetAxisRaw**, and then for **Time.deltaTime**. It's important to understand what's going on here: **Input** is one of the most useful classes provided by Unity, and we can check its settings in the editor (see Figures 3.18 and 3.19).

As we see, by default, the Horizontal axis is tied to the *left* and *right* cursor keys as well as the **A** and **D** keys, while the Vertical axis uses the *up* and *down* or the **W** and **S** keys.

To access these values at runtime, we can then use either *Input.GetAxis* or *Input.GetAxisRaw*.

Both produce values ranging between –1 and 1, but the difference here is that, by using the first method, the value we get is smoothed by the **Sensitivity** setting, making it gradually move from 0 (rest) to either 1 or –1. **GetAxisRaw**, on the other hand, will only output 0 or 1 or –1, making it more suitable for games where we want a precise and immediate effect, like old-school platform games.

Time.deltaTime, instead, is a very commonly used value that returns the time elapsed between frames and is used to ensure that movement is

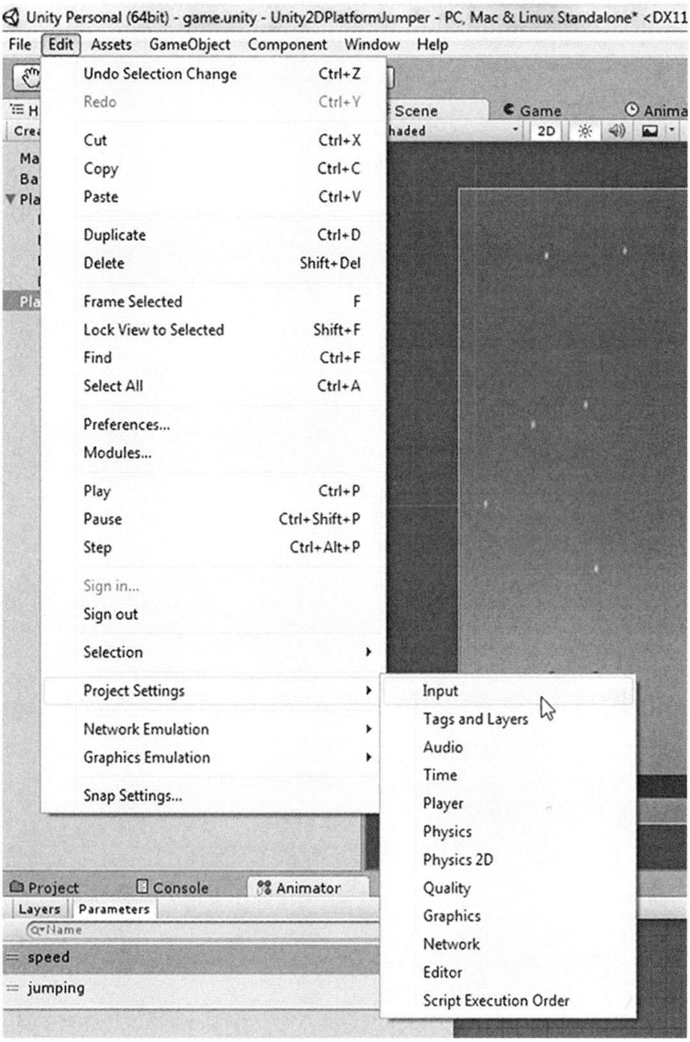

FIGURE 3.18   Within the Unity editor, we can easily access and modify the input settings (Edit/Project Settings/Input).

consistent across frames, that is, we are moving tot units *per second* and not *per frame*.

Once we have the player's input, we need to update the Animator parameters needed to trigger the corresponding animations. By calling the *SetBool* and *SetFloat* methods in the Animator, we can update "jumping" flag and the "speed" variable if any movement is detected in their respective axes.

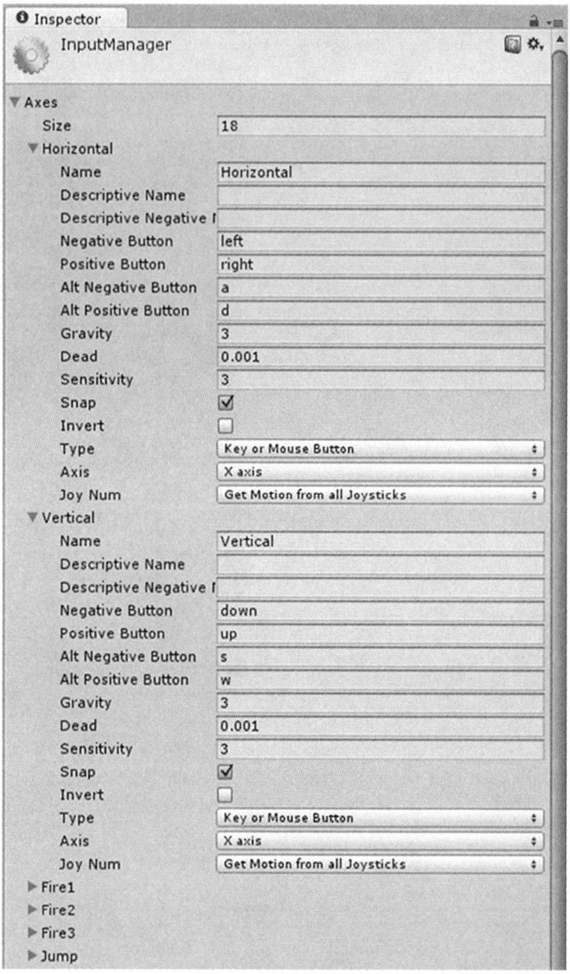

FIGURE 3.19   Via the Input Manager (as displayed in the Inspector), we can associate different axes to specific keys.

The next block of code takes care of flipping the running animation in case we are running left by accessing the *localScale* property of the Player object and changing its *x* value accordingly (we don't need to touch the scaling values on the other axis). Note that, in the *if* condition, we are also checking for the current scaling value so that we don't keep resizing the sprite to the very same value when we keep running in the same direction every frame.

Finally, we can move the player's cat sprite by using the *Translate* method of the *Transform* component and passing it the new *h* and *v* values. Here do note that, if you are using Unity 5.4.0 or newer, the former should also be multiplied by the localScale value to be sure the movement itself isn't mirrored like the animation. (While we don't move along the *z* axis, we still need to write a 0 float value for completeness.)

We can now actually start having a little fun with our prototype and check that everything we did so far works as expected (Figure 3.20)!

The beauty of programming is that it offers countless different ways of doing things. Handling jumping in the way we just did, for example, allows for smooth jumps, with the character jumping higher if we keep the button pressed longer; but, possibly, we may want to handle jumping differently. What about having double jumps, for example? We may also want to use a different control scheme and use a dedicated Jump button instead of relying on the *y* axis.

In that case, we could organize things like this, deleting the v variable in the previous code and writing the following instructions instead (still in *FixedUpdate*):

```
if (Input.GetButtonDown("Jump"))
{
    rb2d.AddForce(Vector2.up * jumpPower);
    pAnim.SetBool("jumping", true);
}
```

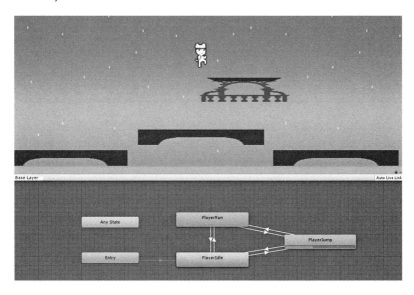

FIGURE 3.20   Testing our game so far. If the cat gets knocked down by the platform, we may want to "freeze" its rotation along the *z* axis (check the **Constraints** field within the Rigidbody component).

```
if (Input.GetButtonUp("Jump"))
{
    pAnim.SetBool("jumping", false);
}
```

Whenever the Jump button is pressed, the first condition will become true, so we add a force along the *y* axis* to the player's *Rigidbody* component proportional to our jumpPower variable (note that you will need to set a higher number than in the earlier example, since we are scaling with Time.deltaTime here).

We also set the jumping flag in the Animator to true, so that we can change animation state accordingly. The gravity force automatically applied to the rigid body will make the character fall down in due time and, when the button is released, we reset the flag to move back to a different animation.

If the player releases the button and then quickly presses it again, the force will be applied again, allowing for a double jump!

Note, also, that there is nothing now preventing the player from tapping the Jump button over and over again, having triple jumps and more. How shall we fix this so that only single and double jumps are allowed? This is actually a good exercise that allows us to introduce tags and collision checking functions.

First off, let's add a new private variable of type *int* and named *jumps* at the beginning of the *PlayerScript* class. This will work as a counter, and we should initialize it within the *Start* function to 0. Then, in FixedUpdate, we should modify our code as follows:

```
if (Input.GetButtonDown("Jump") && jumps < 2)
{
    rb2d.AddForce(Vector2.up * jumpPower);
    pAnim.SetBool("jumping", true);

    jumps++;
}
```

We jump only if the counter is less than 2, and, after the jump, we increment the counter so that it won't be possible to have anything more than a double jump.

---

* Vector2.up identifies a unit vector along the *y* axis (0f, 1f), while AddForce is the most common method for operating over rigidbodies. See https://docs.unity3d.com/ScriptReference/Rigidbody. AddForce.html for more details.

Now, the question is: how and where do we reset the counter? When we hit the ground again on any platform may be a good answer. To do this, we need to be able to easily identify all platforms in the scene, and we can achieve that by using **Tags**.

Tags are nothing more than an identifying label that we can attach to any object to find it easily, whenever needed.

With any object selected, click on the *Tag* drop-down menu in the Inspector and select **Add Tag**, then click on the + sign and name your new tag to **Platform** as in Figure 3.21.

The object selected won't be automatically tagged with the newly defined tag, though, so let's now pick both the *Platform* and *MovingPlatform* prefabs and select the Platform tag for them, as in Figure 3.22. After this, all their instances in the scene will be properly tagged.

The next step is to look for collisions with the platforms.

Unity provides us with an *OnCollisionEnter* method (or *OnCollision Enter2D* in our case, since we are developing a 2D game), which is automatically called when the player's rigid body hits another object's collider.

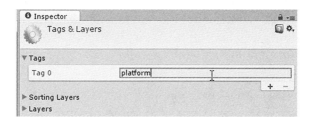

FIGURE 3.21   Adding a new tag.

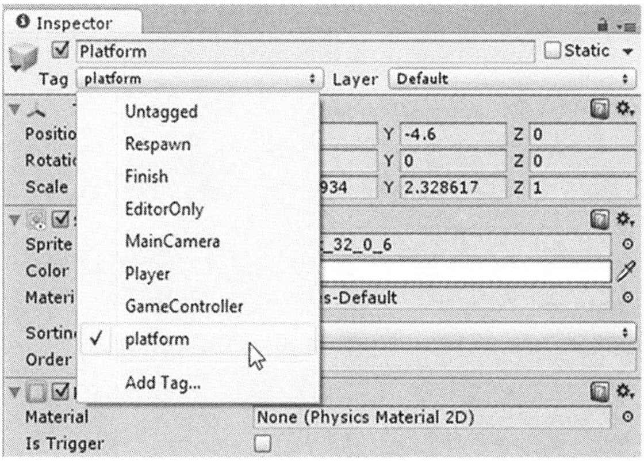

FIGURE 3.22   Tagging the Platform prefab with the "platform" tag.

The method is called with a reference to the colliding object, which we can then check to see whether it is tagged as a platform or not. If so, it means we landed, so we reset the jumps counter allowing the cat to jump again. This is shown in the following code:

```
void OnCollisionEnter2D(Collision2D other)
{
    // if the colliding object is a platform, we
reset the jumping counter
    if (other.gameObject.tag == "platform")
    {
        jumps = 0;
    }
}
```

Running the game now will allow for single and double jumps but nothing more, as the player will be allowed to jump again only after having hit the ground on a platform and not while in the air.

Note also that the moving platform will currently "slide" under the feet of the player. This may actually be an interesting game mechanic to make the level more challenging, but what if we want the platform to behave in a more traditional way and carry the player around?

To achieve this, upon collision, we need to turn the player into a *child* of the MovingPlatform object, and then, when we jump away, we need to restore the player status as a stand-alone object by setting its parent to *null*. The PlayerScript needs to be modified as follows:

```
void OnCollisionEnter2D (Collision2D other) {
  if (other.gameObject.tag == "platform") {
    jumps = 0;
  }
  // if we want the player to move together with the
platform, the latter has to become the player"s
parent.
  if (other.gameObject.name == "MovingPlatform") {
    this.gameObject.transform.parent = other.
gameObject.transform;
  }
}
  void OnCollisionExit2D(Collision2D other) {
    if (other.gameObject.name == "MovingPlatform") {
```

FIGURE 3.23   The *Platform Effector 2D* component. By checking Collider Mask, we can selectively activate (or deactivate) collision with specific layers, while **Use One Way** allows us to define only a range of directions that will be used for the collision detection. This is done by specifying the **Surface Arc** parameter (in this case, 180° means that only collision from the top will be considered, allowing the player to jump on the platform when under it). *Side Friction* and *Bounce* allow for the use of a 2D Physics Material for simulating bouncing and sliding effects on walls and won't be covered here.

```
    this.gameObject.transform.parent = null;
  }
}
```

While playing the game, check in the Hierarchy how the Player object alternates between being stand-alone and being a child to MovingPlatform as we jump on and off it.

Before concluding this chapter, there is just one more concept I would like to introduce: *effectors*.

You may have noticed that the *Box Collider 2D* component has a **Used by Effector** checkbox. What is this for? Among all its various tweaks and improvements, Unity5 also introduced a new set of **Effector** components within the Physics 2D group. By adding a "Platform Effector 2D" for example (Figure 3.23), we can easily implement some typical behaviors of 2D games, like bouncing around, slowly sliding down a wall, or passing through a platform when jumping over it from underneath.

Feel free to add the jump-through behavior to the moving platform if you like, but remember that, for the Effector to be activated, we need to check the corresponding box in the Collider2D component first!

CHAPTER 4

Sound and More

I N OUR PLATFORM GAME, the player can now run and jump with appropriate animations, but we still have several small things to add before we can actually call this a "game." In this section, we will take care of adding sounds, a special object the player needs to collect, and one simple enemy that will move back and forth.

Let's start with sounds. One of the best tools by far for quickly making your own sounds for games having a "retro" feel is Dr. Petter's SFXR, which is freely available from www.drpetter.se/project_sfxr.html. Go ahead and make a jumping sound.

Once you've got a sound you like, save it and drag it into our Sounds project folder. When selected, the Inspector will show us something like Figure 4.1.

Since the jumping sound will be played by our character itself, let's add the *AudioSource* component to the *Player* object, and then pick the jumping sound we just created (Figure 4.2).

Now, we should get back to the *PlayerScript* file to properly access the component and play the SFX.

Like we did earlier for the Rigidbody and Animator components, we start by adding a private variable of type AudioSource:

```
private AudioSource pAudio;
```

Then, in the *Start* function, we can retrieve the actual component:

```
pAudio = GetComponent<AudioSource>();*
```

---

* As we saw in the previous chapter, the 'GetComponent' instruction may be preceded by 'this' and/
or 'GameObject', but these are optional.

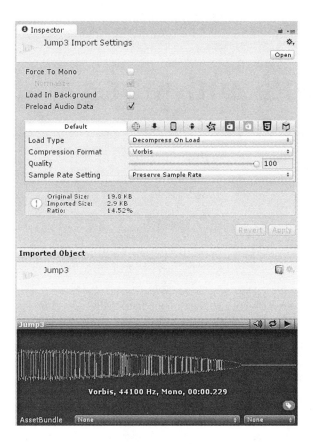

FIGURE 4.1   Properties for a typical sound effect, including a neat preview window. This file was saved as an Ogg Vorbis file, a very common format similar in concept to MP3. Besides these compressed formats, Unity can also import Wave, Aiff, and Tracker modules and then store them on disk in the formats required by the specific platform that we are targeting in our project.

We are now ready to use the *AudioSource* component within our script and play the sound. This is extremely simple to achieve by issuing the command pAudio.Play() when the player is actually jumping, that is, when checking for the jump button press in ***FixedUpdate()***:

```
if (Input.GetButtonDown("Jump") && jumps < 2)
{
  rb2d.AddForce(Vector2.up * jumpPower);
  pAnim.SetBool("jumping", true);
  // let"s have sound!
  pAudio.Play();
```

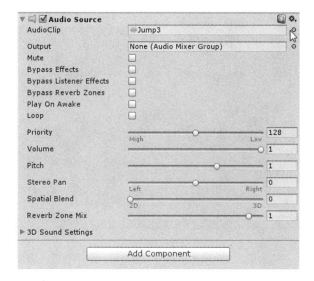

FIGURE 4.2   AudioSource component for the Player object after having selected the audio clip to be later played when jumping.

```
    jumps++;
}
```

Test the game, and check that the sound is being played properly.

Note that, in the scene view, a Loudspeaker icon is now showing over the Player sprite to signify that there is an audio source there. If the icons look too big, we can resize them at will via the *Gizmo* menu, as shown in Figure 4.3.

What we want to do next is to add a coin, star, ring, or whatever we like on top of the moving platform for the player to reach and pick up. This has to move together with the platform, and, when the player reaches it, it should play a nice sound and disappear, like in the old 8 bit classics.

Get a suitable graphic image from websites like OpenGameArt.org or Clker.com (or draw it yourself!) and import it in the Graphics folder. Then drag it INTO the *MovingPlatform* object in the Hierarchy, turning it into a child of that object (Figure 4.4). In this way, the little star will move alongside its parent object, back and forth on the screen.

Once the star has been added to the scene, we need to add a collider to it to later trigger collision events. Let's choose a *Circle Collider 2D* this time, due to the star shape, and check its **Is Trigger** property. Also, note that, while not strictly necessary, for performance reasons Unity suggests that any object that actually moves on the screen should also have a *Rigidbody*

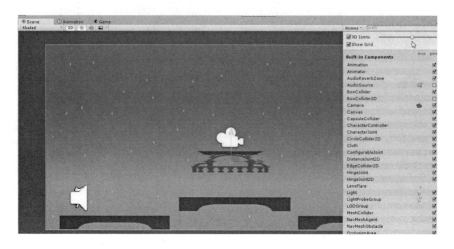

FIGURE 4.3   Changing the size of the 3D icons in the scene via the Gizmo menu.

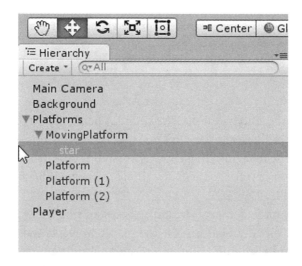

FIGURE 4.4   Turning the star sprite into a child of MovingPlatform.

component attached to it besides the collider. Let's add one now (and do so also to the MovingPlatform prefab) and then check the **Is Kinematic** flag (Figure 4.5): in this way, gravity and other forces won't affect the object, and, instead, we will be free to control it directly ourselves.

We can now add sound. Design a "pickup" sound effect you like in SFXR and import in the scene. Let's add an AudioSource component to the star; but we won't add the audio clip to the former component directly this time, as we will do things slightly differently.

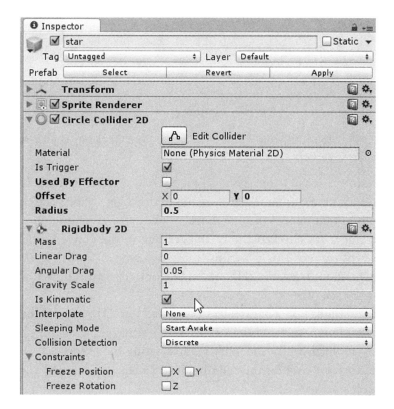

FIGURE 4.5   The Star object with an added Circle Collider 2D and Rigidbody 2D. Note the "Is Kinematic" flag is checked, since we don't want gravity or other forces to affect this particular object, but we will take care of the movement ourselves. If we need to move components up and down to have related components together, just click on the Settings cog for a "Move Up" or "Down" option.

Add a new C# script to the star and call it **StarScript**. We will pick the audio clip as well as handle collisions from there.

The first thing to do in the script is to declare a private variable of type AudioSource to access the Audio component and a public variable of type *AudioClip* to be associated with the specific file we want to play.

```
private AudioSource sAudio;
public AudioClip clip;
```

Save the file, and, back in the scene with the star selected, drag and drop the audio clip to be played into the script's AudioClip variable we just defined, like in Figure 4.6.

FIGURE 4.6   The StarScript is now ready to use the coin pickup sound we made and imported earlier.

Back to the script—in the *Start()* method, we need to actually retrieve the AudioSource component like we did in the other scripts, and then we are ready to take care of the collisions.

Remember we checked the **Is Trigger** flag in the Circle Collider 2D component earlier? This allows us to use two new methods—*OnTrigger-Enter2D* and *OnTriggerExit2D*—when two objects with colliders do "collide" with each other.

Both methods take a parameter of type Collider2D to identify the other object that bumped into them. In this case, our triggering Game object is the player, which we can identify by associating the predefined "Player" tag and then looking for the colliding object's tag, or simply by checking the object's name.

If the star has been touched by the player, we then access the AudioSource component to play the AudioClip using the *PlayOneShotMethod*.

When the player leaves the star, hence triggering the OnTriggerExit2D method, we can destroy the latter object to remove it from the screen.

In the end, *StarScript* should look like the following:

```
using UnityEngine;
using System.Collections;

public class StarScript : MonoBehaviour {
  private AudioSource sAudio;
  public AudioClip clip;

 // Use this for initialization
 void Start () {
     sAudio = this.GetComponent<AudioSource>();
 }

  void OnTriggerEnter2D(Collider2D other) {
    if (other.gameObject.name == "Player")
```

```
    {
      sAudio.PlayOneShot(clip);
    }
  }

  void OnTriggerExit2D(Collider2D other) {
    if (other.gameObject.name == "Player") {
      Destroy(this.gameObject);
    }
  }
}
```

Save everything and play the game now to check that everything works as planned.

To add another challenge, we should now include an enemy roaming a platform in a regular movement pattern. There is nothing new here, as we simply need to go through the same steps we did when adding a platform and animating it by changing its position via the Animator component.

To keep things simple, in the package you can download to check out this project,* I will be using the Plant sprite that comes with the tileset sprite sheet (Figure 4.7) that we are already using, but feel free to look for and import some really bad-guy sprite if you like!

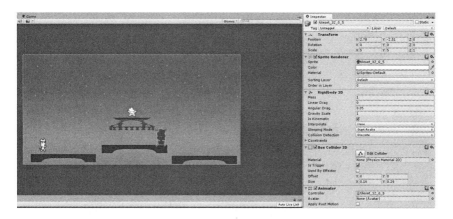

FIGURE 4.7   A plant will roam the central platform and kill the player on touch! Being a moving object, the plant needs a *Rigidbody 2D* component (set to Kinematic) plus a Box Collider 2D (select the *Is Trigger* flag), an Animator object, and its corresponding animation clip.

---

* Check http://ProgramAndPlay.com.

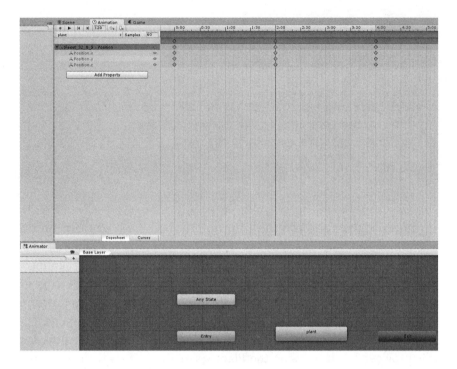

FIGURE 4.8   Animator and Animation components for the plant, manipulating the Transform.Position properties to have it slide back and forth on the platform at a suitable speed.

Once the enemy is placed and its sliding animation defined (Figure 4.8), we need to add a script to handle collision with the player. What we want to achieve now is that, if the player and the plant collide, the former gets moved back to its original position.

We could simply hard code the coordinates we want in the player's script, but that wouldn't be good programming, as it would be too inflexible. A much better way to proceed, instead, is to create a new empty object and then move the player to that object's position. While it won't make any actual difference in this small prototype of ours, if we ever make a bigger game we could reuse this technique to experiment with checkpoints by simply moving the empty object around.

Create an empty object in the Hierarchy and call it "SpawnPoint." Place it where we want the player to appear at the beginning of the game (Figure 4.9). Make a prefab of it, if you like.

Now, we can create a new C# script for the player to handle spawning and collision with enemies (we can call it **PlayerSpawnScript**, for example). It's a

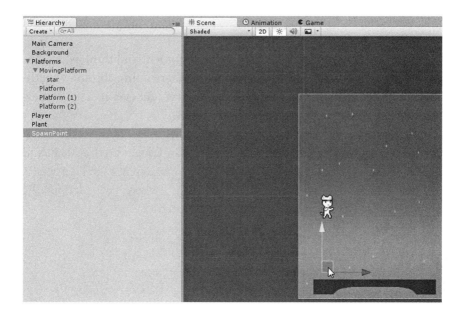

FIGURE 4.9   Using an empty object as a marker for the player's spawning position.

good practice to keep each script small and simple: ideally, we should design our scripts so that each takes care of one task or a few related tasks only.

In this new script, we should first have a public variable of type *Transform* where, once back in the scene view, we associate the empty object we just created. Then, we define a new method call Spawn, from where we reset the player's own position.

The code for spawning is going to be very simple and self-explanatory:

```
public class PlayerSpawnScript : MonoBehaviour {
  public Transform spawn;

 // Use this for initialization
 void Start () {
    PlayerSpawn(spawn);
  }
  void PlayerSpawn() {
    this.transform.position = spawn.position;
  }
}
```

When the script starts, we just call the PlayerSpawn method, where we simply set the *Transform.Position* (which is a Vector3) to the reference position.

Try playing the game now, and move the empty SpawnPosition object around to see the player always appear there.

Before proceeding further, let's stop for a moment and think what happens if we fall out of the screen. Right now, we are doing absolutely nothing, meaning the player will keep falling for ever and ever in a bottomless pit, with Unity tracking its useless coordinates.

Let's fix this right away by adding a new empty object to the scene; call it **Boundary**, add a *Box Collider 2D* (and check its Trigger box), scale it, and place it at the bottom of the level, outside the camera view, as in Figure 4.10.

Then, add a new script to *Boundary*, where we define the OnTriggerEnter2D as follows:

```
public class BoundaryScript : MonoBehaviour {
  void OnTriggerEnter2D(Collider2D other)  {
    if (other.gameObject.name == "Player")
      other.gameObject.SendMessage("PlayerSpawn");
  }
}
```

What happens here is that, when an object triggers the collision with the boundary's own collider, if that object is the player, Boundary will tell Player to call its *PlayerSpawn* method, wherever it is. This is a very important feature that we should remember, as it allows us to call methods written in some script attached to a different object whenever a certain event, like a collision, in this case, occurs.

Test that things work as intended, and then we are ready for the last step of this chapter: handling the collision with this level boss, the fearsome gray plant!

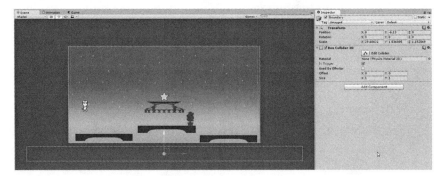

FIGURE 4.10   An empty object having only a collider is placed outside the layout to "catch" the player if he or she falls out of the platforms.

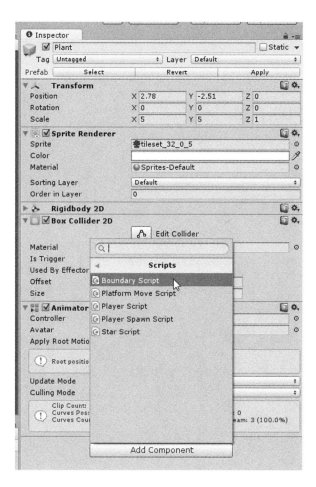

FIGURE 4.11   In checking for a collision between the player and the plant, we don't need to create a new script, but we can actually reuse the one we just defined for the boundary: add the *BoundaryScript* as a component to the Plant object.

Actually, this is very simple task, as it can be handled exactly in the way we just did with Boundary, even by using the very same script as shown in Figure 4.11.

Play test and fine-tune all the variables involved (speed, jump strength, etc.) so that avoiding the plant and reaching the star is challenging but not frustrating.

As an additional exercise, you may want to add a few more sounds to be played when the player respawns after dying.

CHAPTER 5

Scoring and Final Touches

O UR SIMPLE PLATFORMER PROTOTYPE is now taking shape; however, to complete the playing loop, we still need to set a proper scoring system and winning condition. Don't forget, scoring points is not only the most basic way to reward players for playing successfully but also one of the most effective to actually provide a gratifying experience. Not many people will play games if there are no ways to measure and compare their skills, setting and beating their own or other people's records!

Currently, our prototype restarts if the cat dies by either falling out of the screen or being hit by the plant, and the cat can collect the little star on the floating platform. What we want to add now is an exit that appears after having picked up the star: the player needs to reach it to, ideally, win the level and access the next area of the game. We also want to add a score to be displayed on the screen, to be updated every time a star is collected.

For the exit, we can use the moon sprite we have in the already imported tileset (these are just placeholders we are using for quick prototyping). Once again, you can surely get more suitable graphics around the web, just be sure to always credit the source/author according to the original license!

Create a new empty object in the Hierarchy and add a Sprite Renderer component to it, or just drag and drop the moon image from the Assets/ Graphics folder into the Hierarchy to create the new object. Name it **Exit**, scale it properly, and place it somewhere opposite to the player (Figure 5.1).

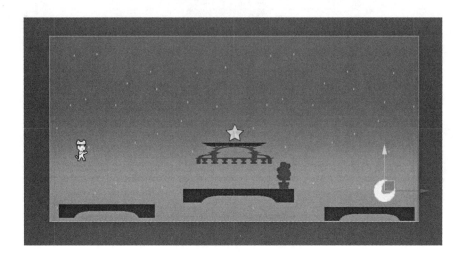

FIGURE 5.1   The game layout after having added a moon that will appear only after the star has been picked up to magically teleport the cat to a new challenge (well, sort of!).

Turn the exit moon into a prefab, delete the original moon from the scene, and then bring into the scene another *SpawnPoint* prefab. Call this **ExitPoint**, and place it where the moon was. The exit will be created at this very position by the Star object in its *OnTriggerEnter2D* method.

To achieve this, we need to add two more public variables in *StarScript*: one for the *Exit* game object and one for its position, the SpawnPoint.

```
// the exit sprite
public GameObject exit;
public Transform exitPoint;
```

Once the file has been saved and the corresponding objects linked in the Inspector window (Figure 5.2), OnTriggerEnter2D needs to be modified by adding a call to the *Instantiate* method. This function allows us to add a new object to the scene and needs three parameters: the object we want to create as first parameter (the exit sprite in this case), its spawning position as second (this is a Vector3), followed by its rotation (we can use the default **Quaternion.identity** here, since no rotation is needed*).

```
void OnTriggerEnter2D(Collider2D other) {
    if (other.gameObject.name == "Player") {
```

---

* In a nutshell, quaternions are angles used to identify an object rotation.

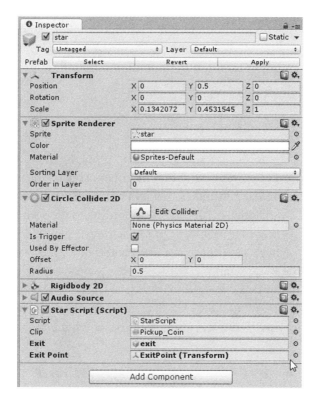

FIGURE 5.2   Modifying the StarScript to handle the spawning of the Exit object at a specific location.

```
        sAudio.PlayOneShot(clip);

        // we can now instantiate the exit sprite
        Instantiate (exit, exitPoint.
position, Quaternion.identity);
    }
}
```

If we test the game now, upon reaching the star this will spawn the exit moon before self-destroying.

Reaching the exit won't do anything yet, though, and this is our next task.

Moving to a new level means loading a new scene. Since, in this prototype, we won't actually have any other levels (designing a few more would be a terrific exercise, though!), we will simply reload the current scene to start again. This can be achieved with a simple command using the *LoadLevel* method of the *Application* object as shown here:

```
void OnTriggerEnter2D(Collider2D other)
{
  if (other.gameObject.name == "Player")
  {
    Application.LoadLevel("game");
  }
}
```

LoadLevel is another very handy method that we should remember, and we can use it to access a new scene by either using the new scene name (as in this case) or using its index, that is, a number starting from 0, which is automatically assigned by the engine according to the scene build order (we can specify these via *File Menu/Build Settings*).

That's all we need to write in the new ExitScript.cs file that we have to associate to the Exit prefab.

Now, the score. This allows us to introduce Unity's graphical user interface (GUI) system. Like in Figure 5.3, create a new Game object by selecting the UI and then Text entry from the drop-down menu.

FIGURE 5.3   Adding a new Text UI element to display the game score.

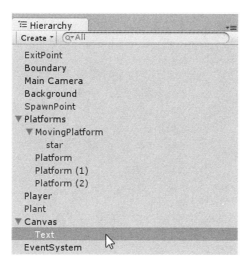

FIGURE 5.4   The newly created Canvas element and its child object Text.

Unity will then add the *Text* element as a child of a more general *Canvas* object (which is going to contain any GUI element), together with an *EventSystem* object (Figure 5.4).

The GUI panel is being displayed in its own 2D space, independently from the rest of the Game scene (whether 3D or 2D), and, if we now select the newly created Text object and focus on it by pressing *F* while the cursor is on the scene, and then zoom out a little, we will see the available GUI screen area delimited by a white frame.

The Text object also has its set of components visible in the Inspector, where we can start customizing its appearance, such as font, color, size, and actual text (Figure 5.5). Let's call it *Score*, make it white, center its alignment, and increase the font size.

If the text suddenly disappears, don't worry: this simply means its size has outgrown the original text window. Select the *Transform* tool (Figure 5.6), and change it accordingly (Figure 5.7).

Figure 5.5 shows also another component, *Rect Transform*, which is very important for shaping and positioning any GUI element properly. By clicking on its small rectangle (Figure 5.8), a new menu will appear where we can choose to anchor the object to a specific part of the screen, as well as change its pivot point (by pressing Shift) and its position (by also pressing Alt). In our case, if we decide to place the score in the upper edge of the screen, centered, we can press both Shift and Alt and then click on the corresponding position, as in Figure 5.9.

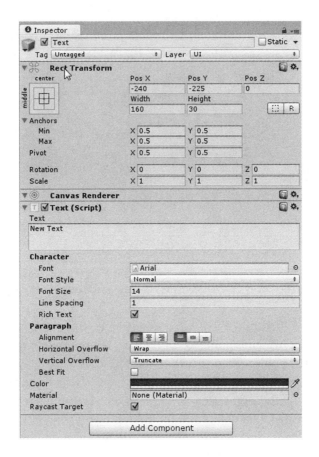

FIGURE 5.5   The default components associated to the Text UI object.

FIGURE 5.6   Use the Transform tool to resize and move the Text window.

If we play the game now, we should see the text appear where we positioned it. To be sure that it is also properly anchored, try resizing the Game window: if the text maintains its position, we did everything correctly; otherwise, try again to anchor it to the desired position via the Rect Transform component in the *Inspector*.

How do we make this display a game score, then? For example, we want the game to start displaying a value of 0, which should be updated to 1 as

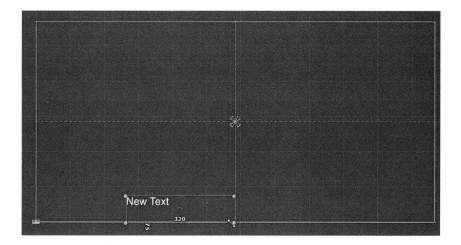

FIGURE 5.7 After clicking on the Transform tool, we can freely resize the rectangle framing the text and move it around the area by clicking and dragging the circle in the middle.

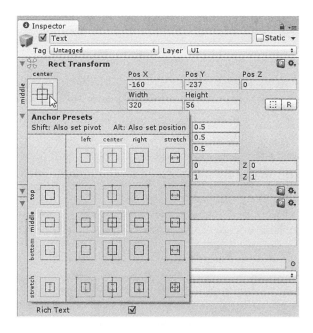

FIGURE 5.8 The Rect Transform component.

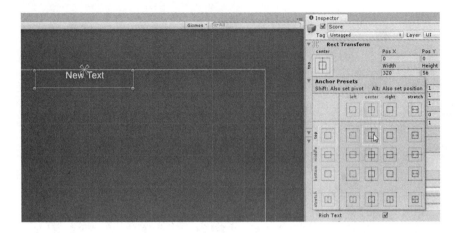

FIGURE 5.9   Positioning and anchoring the Text element to the upper edge of the screen.

soon as the player reaches the star. To achieve this, we can create a new *empty object* in the *Hierarchy*, name it *ScoreObject*, and add a new C# script to it, *ScoreScript*.

When editing the script (shown in the listing that follows), the first thing we should do is add a line,

```
using UnityEngine.UI;
```

which is needed to handle anything UI related. Then, we need to declare a public variable of type Text, which we will link to the existing *Score* Text field by dragging that into the resulting Inspector property.

This is followed by something new: a private static variable. The *static* keyword allows for the variable to be used as a global: that is, there will be only one instance of it, which will be accessible to other objects. Most importantly, it will maintain its value through the various calls and not be reinstantiated every time the script is called.

This is obviously very powerful, but also dangerous, as any script can change the variable and potentially affect anything else that uses it, making debugging a nightmare if something goes wrong; so, use static variables with care.

In the *Start()* method, we can initialize the variable to 0 and then pass it to the Text object for displaying it. To do so, we need first to convert the numeric value using the *ToString()* method. Use the same approach in the only other function we need to add to the script—a method that other objects can call specifying the incremental score value, passed as a parameter of type *int*.

```
using UnityEngine;
using System.Collections;
// remember to add this whenever using the UI!
using UnityEngine.UI;

public class ScoreScript : MonoBehaviour {
    // the text object within the Canvas we want to
update.
    public Text scoreField;
    // static variable
    static int score;
    // Use this for initialization
    void Start () {
    // start the game with a score of 0
    score = 0;
    scoreField.text = score.ToString();
    }
    // Update the score field
    void UpdateScore (int value) {
      // update the score by the amount specified
      score += value;
      scoreField.text = score.ToString();
      }
}
```

Once the script is written, we can go back to StarScript.cs to finish things.

First, let's add a new object,

```
public GameObject scoreObj;
```

that we will associate to the newly created ScoreObject in the usual way.*

FIGURE 5.10 The platforming prototype, now with a working score at the top of the screen!

Once the reference is set, in OnTriggerEnter2D method we just have to add the following line,

```
scoreObj.SendMessage("UpdateScore",1);
```

so that, when we check for a collision with the player's sprite, we can call *UpdateScore* in the ScoreObject, hence updating the Text element in the UI.

In summary, we have first set a Text object using the UI. This is referenced by a Score object that will be accessed by any in-game object that will require the score to be updated (just the star in our very basic platforming prototype).

If we play the game and reach the star, now not only will the moon-shaped exit magically appear, but also the score will be incremented from 0 to 1 (Figure 5.10).

It's your turn now to keep exploring a little bit, and make the prototype a little more interesting and complex: More enemies? Stars? Levels? You decide! In fact, you now have all the elements to actually build a simple full game: in these first five chapters, we have explored a lot of ground: using prefabs, adding objects, animating and moving them around a scene via Unity's unique Mecanim system, for example. We also saw collision detection and triggers and how to play sounds, spawn objects, display text via the UI system, have objects call each other methods, and more.

All these are the fundamental blocks that you need to be familiar with to start your game development journey in Unity, so take your time to understand how these work together in the example we have built so far, and then proceed to the next chapters, where we will build a full game suitable for mobile platforms!

II

Building a Match 3 Game for PC and Mobile

CHAPTER 6

Game and Music Managers

We are now ready to develop a small but complete 2D project. As a case study, we will design a simple match-3 type of game, where we have to match rows or columns of gems in a well-known game mechanic that has been a staple of casual gaming since *Bejeweled* by PopCap Games hit our computers in 2001.*

Matching sequences of items is a simple concept that, nonetheless, will allow us to understand how grid-based games can be implemented (and many games are based on grids!), while also exploring additional Unity features like layers and raycasts. Also, our game will start on a PC for easier testing, but we will later turn it into an Android package to see how the transition to mobile works.

First of all, let's think of the overall game manager to handle the various scenes that must be included to build the actual game skeleton: we want a Splash screen to automatically transit to a Main Menu, an Option screen, the screen where the actual game is played, and, last but not least, a Game Over screen. They should all be linked to each other like in Figure 6.1, and we also want to implement an audio manager to play some background music throughout the various screens.

Start a new 2D project in Unity, and name it in any way you'd like to call our upcoming game.

---

* See https://en.wikipedia.org/wiki/Bejeweled_(series) for more information.

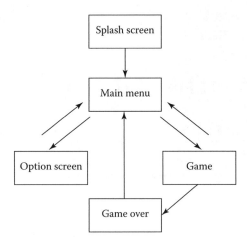

FIGURE 6.1   Our first step is to implement a game manager able to handle different scenes defining the overall game structure.

Our first task will be to make the Splash screen. This will be a perfect place to show our logo, instantiate a few things (like the music manager), and smoothly transit to the game's Main Menu.

Add a few folders, named "Scenes," "Scripts," "Graphics," "Fonts," "Prefabs," and "Sounds." Save the current scene as "00 Splash" (numbering scenes is a good idea to order them easily later), and let's start scouting for some images and assets.

Remember that there are plenty of resources online to get free assets and start prototyping right away. For example, at the moment of writing, the following are among those worth checking out:

- www.opengameart.org (both 2D and 3D artwork plus sounds)
- www.openmusicarchive.org
- www.freesound.org
- www.freesfx.co.uk
- www.clker.com (clip art)
- www.dafont.com (fonts)

Let's start by picking an image you would like to use for the Splash screen (I will be using my own logo, but of course you can pick anything else), a sound effect you like (e.g., I will be using one of the SFX available here: http://www.freesfx.co.uk/soundeffects/magic/), and a good-looking font (like http://www.dafont.com/snaphand.font), and place everything in the corresponding folders.

In the starting scene, let's add a new Game object from the User Interface (UI)/Image menu and call it "Logo." As we know from the previous chapters, this will be created together with a *Canvas* and *EventSystem* to handle any UI element within the scene. Import the previously downloaded logo image as the source image of the object, and place this in the center of the screen, doing any small change needed to make it look good. If you want the image to scale up or down together with the screen, be sure to set the **UI Scale Mode** to **Scale with Screen Size** in the **Canvas Scaler** component of the canvas accessible via the Inspector.

We can now proceed to add a short introductory text under the logo, for example, "<Your Name> Presents...." Just add a new game object from the UI/Text menu and select the font we downloaded previously, adjusting its position, size, and color to match your logo (Figure 6.2).

The next step is to associate the sound to a new empty object or to the main camera. We don't want it to loop, but we want it to "play on awake," that is, when the scene is loaded. Testing the scene now will show the logo, text, and sound, but, obviously, nothing else will happen yet: what the Splash scene has to do is to wait just for a few seconds and then automatically load the next scene, "Main Menu."

Create a new script in the Scripts folder, name it **GameManager**, and open it for editing.

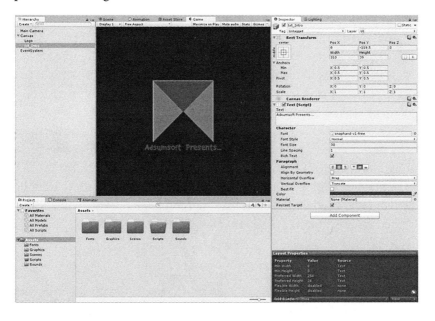

FIGURE 6.2   Setting up a Splash screen with a custom logo and text.

To handle scene transitions, we are going to use Unity's built-in *SceneManager* class, and to do so we need to include the corresponding library first:

```
using UnityEngine.SceneManagement;
```

The SceneManager class has several handy methods, and we are now going to use its **LoadScene** function. This can be used by specifying either the name of the scene that has to be loaded or an index specified in the build order, plus an additional parameter to tell the engine whether it is closing all existing scenes ("single") or loading the new scene while keeping the current ones in memory ("additive").

We also need to declare a couple of variables: a public float *delay* that will store the time, in seconds, that we will be waiting before loading the new scene, and a private int *index* variable to store the value of the current scene, enabling us to load the next one. We will specify the exact scene order later, via the *Build* settings. The index variable has to be *static*, meaning that it will be shared by any instance of the script and any object that will reference it.

```
public float delay;
static int index;
```

Now, while we could simply load the new scene explicitly in the *Start* function and consider the job done, we want our script not just to handle this scene transition from the Splash screen to the Main Menu but also to help us in loading all future scenes in a variety of ways, so we should start writing our code with a more general approach in mind and have a dedicated method for loading the next scene.

This also means that we want the *GameManager* object to be persistent across all our scenes in the game. To achieve this, we need to add a specific command during initialization: *DontDestroyOnLoad*.

The **Start()** method will then be like the following, where we initialize index and call the **LoadNextScene()** method after the value, in seconds, specified in delay, thanks to the **Invoke** function:

```
void Start () {
    DontDestroyOnLoad(this.gameObject);
    index = 0;
    Invoke ("LoadNextScene", delay);
}
```

Then, the actual **LoadNextScene()** can be written like this:

```
public void LoadNextScene() {
  SceneManager.LoadScene(++index, LoadSceneMode.
Single);
        }
```

Notice how we are passing the index here. We want to increment the variable so that we now load the scene having index equal to 1. In this regard, there is a subtle difference between writing "++index" and "index++." The former syntax increments the variable first and then uses it in the call. If we wrote "index++" instead, we would have simply reloaded the existing scene, because index would have been used with its original value of 0 at first and only incremented later, when it was too late.

At the moment, the whole script will look like this:

```
using UnityEngine;
using System.Collections;
using UnityEngine.SceneManagement;
public class GameManager : MonoBehaviour {
  public float delay;
  static int index;
  void Start () {
        DontDestroyOnLoad(this.gameObject);
        index = 0;
         Invoke ("LoadNextScene", delay);
      }
      public void LoadNextScene() {
         SceneManager.LoadScene(++index,
LoadSceneMode.Single);
              }
  }
```

Attach the script to a new empty Game object, also named **GameManager**, for consistency, and turn this into a prefab by dragging it into the Prefab folder we created earlier.

Now, add a new scene to the project, calling it **01 Main Menu**. Since we are already in the process of creating new scenes, let's complete the work here and add some scenes, **02 Options**, **03 GameOver**, and **04 Game**, which we can then include in the Build settings (Figure 6.3).

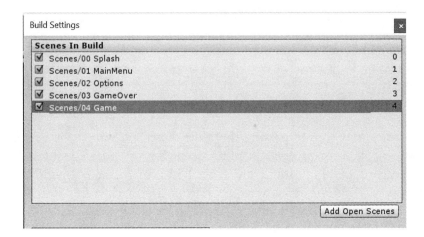

FIGURE 6.3   All the scenes in our upcoming match-3 game. Notice the index on the far right.

You may wonder why we indexed and inserted the Game Over scene before the actual game. The reason is, in case our game will feature several levels each in its own scene, it would be a good idea to have all the levels indexed in sequence, from four onward, so that we can easily call the next scene in the way we just saw; so, having the Game Over indexed before the game levels may make things a little more organized.

If we actually build the game now, the Splash screen will work properly, playing its jingle and then moving to the blank screen that is currently the Main Menu (the scene identified by the index 1).

It's high time to design the Main Menu now. Open the scene and add a new Text UI element, calling it "Title." Set the font and write the name of your game (I will write "Jem Matcher" here), positioning the text somewhere in the center or upper half of the canvas. If you think you may reuse this in future in some other scene, turn it into a prefab.

Clickable buttons can be done in different ways. For example, for our "Options" and "Start" buttons, we want to design them as a text using the same font that we used for the title, with the color changing when the mouse runs over them and clicks them. To achieve this, add a new UI/Text element and name it "Options." After setting up the font, its size, and its initial color in the Inspector, click "Add Component" and add a UI/Button to it. That's all we need to have clickable texts and navigate across the game scenes. Among its options, the new component allows us to set different types of transitions (including sprite swapping or animations), but here, having just a text acting

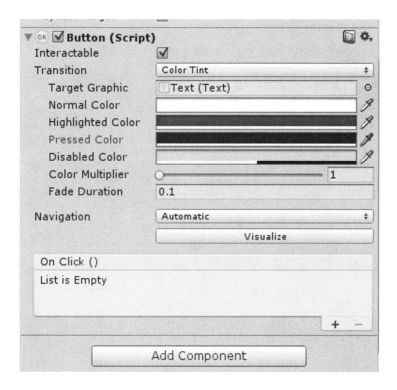

FIGURE 6.4   Adding the Button component to a Text object and setting up different colors to identify its highlighted and pressed states.

as a button, we will simply use "Color Tint:" set appropriate "highlighted" and "pressed" colors (Figure 6.4), like red and blue, for example.

To take action when clicked, we need to specify the button's event list, shown at the bottom of the component. We want it to access the GameManager object and call the *LoadNextScene* method. To do this, click on the + in the *OnClick()* event, and then click on the dot to select the object. In the corresponding window (Figure 6.5), look for the GameManager prefab (in the Assets tab) and select it. Finally, in the Function drop-down menu, look for the GameManager script and then our LoadNextScene method (Figure 6.6).

Turn the Options button into a prefab (which we may rename as **TextButton** to make it sound more general purpose).

Don't forget to set the canvas **UI Scale Mode** to **Scale with Screen Size**, and then feel free to go back to the Splash scene to run it: after the predefined delay, it will move to Main Menu (scene 1), and now, when we

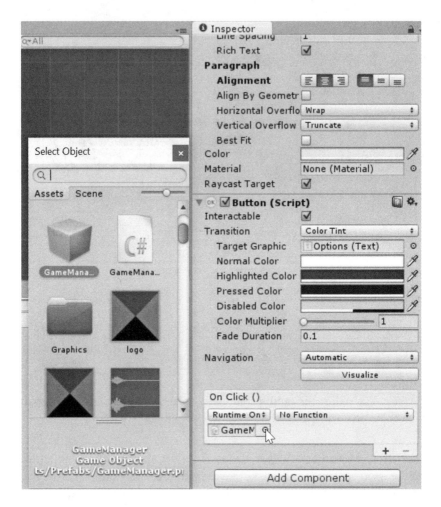

FIGURE 6.5   The OnClick event for the button has to be associated with the GameManger object*...

click on "Options," it will move to the corresponding blank Options scene having index equal to 2.

Before starting to work on the other scenes, we should add a couple more text-based buttons to our Main Menu first, like **Start** and **Quit**. Set them up by using the freshly made "TextButton" prefab. But what functions shall we link them to in GameManager? We need to go back to the script and expand it accordingly. Loading a new scene by name can be

---

* A common error here is to directly specify the script itself, but this will not allow us to access its methods. We need to associate the actual object having the script as one of its components for the OnClick() event to work properly and reach the desired callback function.

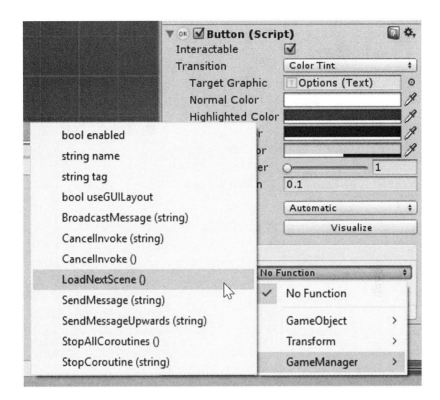

FIGURE 6.6   ... and then, we have to call the LoadNextScene function in the GameManager script we wrote earlier. This will be executed whenever we click the text-based button.

done in a very similar way to LoadNextScene(), where we have the name passed as a parameter:

```
public void LoadSceneByName(string name) {
    SceneManager.LoadScene(name, LoadSceneMode.
    Single);
}
```

The parameter has to be passed from the event specified in the Inspector for the specific button, like in Figure 6.7.

For the Quit button, we can write another very straightforward method, relying on the Quit() method of the Application class:

```
public void Quit() {
    Application.Quit ();
}
```

FIGURE 6.7 We want the Start button to call LoadSceneByName specifying "04 Game" (i.e., the scene name) as the method's parameter of type string.

Our Main Menu should now look something like Figure 6.8, and, if we build and run the project as a PC game, we will be able to move from the Splash screen to the Menu and, from there, either quit the application or move to the Option screen.

We now need to complete the navigation system between the scenes: Options and Start should be able to bring us back to the Main Menu, and, for testing purposes, we should also have a button from the Game scene leading us to the Game Over screen. The latter should then have a button heading back to the Main Menu.

We already have all the knowledge to complete these small tasks, but let's do a couple of things in a slightly different way now, for example, by also using the actual Button object provided by the UI to see how this works.

Load the Option scene,* add the game title as a Text object, and then pick the "UI/Button" element in the "Game Object" drop-down menu to

---

* If Unity adds a default skybox and you would like to remove it for a 2D game, simply open the "Window" drop-down menu and select the "Lighting" tab and then "Scene." Once there, set the "Environment Lighting Skybox" option to "none."

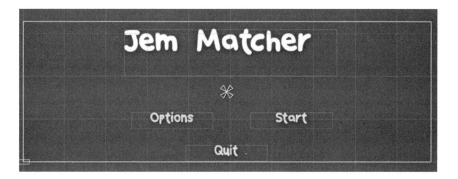

FIGURE 6.8   The Main Menu scene for the upcoming Jem Matcher game, showing text-based buttons for moving to an Option screen, starting the game, or closing the application.

add it to the canvas (Figure 6.9). As we see from the Inspector, the Button object is nothing more than an image plus a text and the same button component we used earlier. Change the text to "Back" in the child Text object, and then change the highlighted and pressed color of the button component in the parent object.

What method should we associate to its OnClick() event? For sure, we could use the already written *LoadSceneByName* method, passing it the name 01 Main Menu as parameter, but this scene has been placed right after the Main Menu in the build order, so we can complete our script by

FIGURE 6.9   A very simple Option screen with no actual options yet (we will add them later) and featuring only the title of the game and a button to go back to the Main Menu to test the game navigation system.

adding one more method to quickly access the scene having the previous index:

```
public void LoadPreviousScene() {
      SceneManager.LoadScene(--index,
      LoadSceneMode.Single)
}
```

For completeness, we could also add one last method in the script to load a scene having its index as an integer parameter in input: we would then be free to choose any possible method in our game according to specific needs and situations. Writing and testing this last function is left as a simple exercise for the reader.

Back in the Inspector, link the new *LoadPreviousScene* method to the *Back* button OnClick() event like we did earlier. It may be a good idea to turn this into a prefab as well.

Similarly, in the *Game* scene, add another "Back" button to head back to the Main Menu, plus a temporary "Game Over" button to head over to the final scene. Use either text- or image-based buttons, and load the Menu scene by passing its name or index to the appropriate method in the *GameManager* script. Do the same for the Game Over screen.

With the infrastructure for scene navigation done, we can move on to implementing a music manager component that will play different tracks according to different scenes. In our case, we want a first track playing in the *Main Menu* and *Options*, another playing during the actual Game scene, and one more for the *Game Over*. Get a couple of free or public domain (PD) songs you deem suitable for our game. Here, I will be using the following tracks: "Sunrise over Clear Skies" (http://opengameart.org/content/sunrise), "Vicegrip of Pursuit" (http://opengameart.org/content/pursuit), and "Alone" (http://opengameart.org/content/alone) by Sudocolon for the Main Menu, In-game and Game Over scenes, respectively.

Import the tracks into the Unity project, add an *AudioSource* component to our GameManager object, and create a new C# script named **Music Manager** to be added to the *GameManager* as well.

Start editing *Music Manager*. First of all, we need to define an array of audio clips:

```
public AudioClip[] tracks;
```

FIGURE 6.10   Note how audio clips to be played are defined not in the AudioSource component directly but in our own MusicManager script via a public array named "Tracks." Since we are planning for three tracks in our game, define the Size parameter accordingly, and then drag and drop the music files we imported earlier. Elements 0, 1, and 2 should be referencing the music for the Main and Options screens, the actual game, and the Game Over screen, respectively.

This needs to be public, since we are associating the actual clips via the Inspector (Figure 6.10).

Back in the script, we should define a couple of private variables now: one to access the AudioSource component and one to store the index of the track currently being played. The latter will allow us to keep playing a track without restarting it (e.g., when moving from the Main Menu to the Options screen and back).

```
AudioSource music;
int current;
```

These variables are going to be initialized right away in the Start() method, with *current* set to −1 to indicate that we aren't playing anything yet (the first track has index 0 in the array), while *music* is actually set to retrieve the AudioSource component in the very same GameManager object it belongs to.

```
void Start () {
        // currently, we aren"t playing any music
        current = -1;
        // retrieving the AudioSource component of
the GameManager object
        music = GetComponent<AudioSource>();
}
```

At the heart of the script we have a new method, *PlayTrack*, having in input an integer parameter specifying the index of the *tracks* array to be played.

This function has first to check that the track requested is different from the one being played and, if so, stop the music, select the new song, set the *loop* flag to true, and, finally, proceed to play it. This can all be achieved in a very straightforward way:

```
public void PlayTrack(int i)
{
        // start the music only if we requested for
a different track
        if (current != i) {
                current = i;
                music.Stop ();
                music.clip = tracks [i];
                music.loop = true;
                music.Play ();
        }
}
```

To summarize, the whole script will now look like the following:

```
using UnityEngine;
using System.Collections;
public class MusicManager: MonoBehaviour {
        // music tracks to be played across the game.
```

```
      public AudioClip[] tracks;
      // AudioSource is needed to play music and
sounds.
      AudioSource music;
      // which track are we playing?
      int current;
      // Use this for initialization
      void Start () {
            // currently, we aren"t playing any music
            current = -1;
            // retrieving the AudioSource component of
the GameManager object
            music = GetComponent<AudioSource>();
      }
      public void PlayTrack(int i)
      {
            // start the music only if we requested for
a different track
            if (current != i) {
                  // update current variable, then
play new clip
                  current = i;
                  music.Stop ();
                  music.clip = tracks [i];
                  music.loop = true;
                  music.Play ();
            }
      }
}
```

The PlayTrack method needs to be called from each scene where we want to start playing a new music track. To organize this, let's start by loading the *Main Menu* scene and add a new empty object there, calling it *MusicPlayer*. Create also a new MusicPlayer script and add it to the object. This script needs a public integer variable, through which we will request a particular track as specified in the Inspector, plus a private *GameObject* to access the existing GameManager.

In the Start() method, we can then find GameManager and call the PlayTrack method specifying the song we want:

```
      // the index of the music track to be played
      public int track;
```

```
    // the GameManager object
    GameObject manager;
    // Use this for initialization
    void Start () {
    // Find GameManager and call its PlayTrack
method with the desired track
        manager = GameObject.Find ("GameManager");
        manager.GetComponent<MusicManager>
().PlayTrack (track);
    }
```

Turn this object into a prefab and add the MusicPlayer object also to all the other scenes where we want to start playing one of the songs (i.e., Game and Game Over), specifying the track value accordingly (i.e., 0 for the object in Main Menu and Options, 1 in Game, and 2 in Game Over).

Once done, play the game and check that the right music is played in the right scenes.

However, no matter how beautiful the music for our game is, some players will always prefer the sound of silence, especially if playing on a mobile device, so this is a good moment to actually go back to the Options scene and add the possibility to switch off the music completely or modify its volume at will. Let's add two more objects to the canvas there: one *Toggle* and one *Slider*, both under the UI category. We can leave the default names or change them to "MusicToggle" and "MusicSlider," if we prefer. Add, also, a small Text object to be placed above the slider to describe its function, like in Figure 6.11. This can be added as a child to the slider to be sure their relative position remains consistent across different resolutions.

Selecting the toggle or the slider will show several fields in the Inspector for us to modify, allowing us to customize the look and feel of each UI element. Feel free to have fun exploring the possibilities, though for simplicity's sake, for our game example I will be modifying only the slider's **Pressed color** to a bright yellow and will leave all other graphics and parameters to their default values. Our slider will then look quite plain and move between 0 and 1, but the important thing to note is the "On Value Changed" tab at the bottom of the component, where we could associate the appropriate callback method to be called when the specific event is triggered (i.e., the float value of the slider or the Boolean value of the toggle are modified by the user in the game).

We need now to proceed with the appropriate script. Once this is done, we could then associate the relevant methods directly from the Inspector,

FIGURE 6.11   The Options scene after having added a toggle for switching music on/off and a slider for changing its volume.

like we did earlier when handling the various buttons to navigate in between the scenes; but this time, let's do things a bit differently, as it is actually more instructive to handle everything programmatically.

Create a new empty object, call it **Music Options**, and add a new C# script to it with the same name. Open it and add the following variables to reference the Slider and Toggle objects in the scene, plus a GameObject to access the omnipresent GameManager:

```
// reference to the Slider
public Slider volumeSlider;
// reference to the music on/off toggle
public Toggle checkbox;
// the GameManager object
GameObject manager;
```

Since we are using UI elements, we also need to remember to add the following line at the beginning of the script:

```
using UnityEngine.UI;
```

We can then initialize all these in the Start() function; for manager, we simply need to find the GameManager to access it later in the script:

```
manager = GameObject.Find ("GameManager");
```

However, for *volumeSlider* and *checkbox*, we need to be a bit more careful. For these, in fact, we need not only to retrieve the relevant values from the AudioSource component in GameManager, but also to set up the callback method to be activated whenever the corresponding UI element changes.

For the slider, these steps can be achieved in the following way, first retrieving the *volume* level so that the slider position starts in the right place and then adding a listener to kick in whenever the slider value changes, delegating a new method (here called **VolumeChange**) to take the necessary actions:

```
    volumeSlider.value = manager.
GetComponent<AudioSource> ().volume;
    volumeSlider.onValueChanged.AddListener
(delegate {VolumeChange ();});
```

For the checkbox, we proceed in a very similar way: here, we have first to retrieve the *mute* flag from AudioSource and activate/deactivate the UI element accordingly:

```
        checkbox.isOn = !manager.
GetComponent<AudioSource> ().mute;
```

We also want to give the checkbox control over the slider; that is, if the checkbox is off, we should deactivate the slider as well, since moving it wouldn't make much sense without music being played. The code will be like this:

```
    volumeSlider.enabled = checkbox.isOn;
```

And, last, we can add a listener to call a new method, **AudioToggle**, whenever the checkbox value changes:

```
        checkbox.onValueChanged.AddListener
(delegate {AudioToggle();});
```

The two new methods, *VolumeChange* and *AudioToggle*, are pretty straightforward, with the first simply matching the volume level to the slider position:*

---

* Note that both are set between 0 and 1 by default, so no scaling is necessary.

```
public void VolumeChange() {
        manager.GetComponent<AudioSource> ().volume
= volumeSlider.value;
    }
```

The second is just a little bit more complicated. Here, we need to evaluate the checkbox's *isOn* flag and then mute/unmute the AudioSource component via its *Mute* flag. When the former is true, the latter must be false, and vice versa. We also want to enable or disable the slider accordingly:

```
    public void AudioToggle() {
        if (!checkbox.isOn) {
            manager.GetComponent<AudioSource>
().mute = true;
            volumeSlider.enabled = false;
        } else {
            manager.GetComponent<AudioSource>
().mute = false;
            volumeSlider.enabled = true;
        }
    }
```

That's it! The whole script will then look like the following:

```
using UnityEngine;
using System.Collections;
// we are using UI components so don"t forget about
this!
using UnityEngine.UI;

public class MusicOptions : MonoBehaviour {
    // reference to the Slider
    public Slider volumeSlider;
    // reference to the music on/off toggle
    public Toggle checkbox;
    // the GameManager object
    GameObject manager;

    // Use this for initialization
    void Start () {
        // get the GameManager first
        manager = GameObject.Find ("GameManager");
```

```
            //we add a listener to the slider and
invoke a method when the value changes.
            volumeSlider.value = manager.
GetComponent<AudioSource> ().volume;
            volumeSlider.onValueChanged.AddListener
(delegate {VolumeChange ();});

            // set variables according to last
AudioSource state.
            checkbox.isOn = !manager.
GetComponent<AudioSource> ().mute;
            // should the slider be active? i.e. music
not muted? Depends on the checkbox own status
            volumeSlider.enabled = checkbox.isOn;

            // adding a listener to Toggle to trigger
the corresponding method.
            checkbox.onValueChanged.AddListener
(delegate {AudioToggle();});
        }

            public void VolumeChange() {
            // we need to access the AudioSource
component of MusicManager to update the playing
volume.
            // Both values are between 0 and 1 so no
scaling is necessary.
            manager.GetComponent<AudioSource> ().volume
= volumeSlider.value;
        }

    public void AudioToggle() {
            // if not selected, mute the audio and
disable the slider
            // otherwise do the opposite
            if (!checkbox.isOn) {
                manager.GetComponent<AudioSource>
().mute = true;
                volumeSlider.enabled = false;
            } else {
                manager.GetComponent<AudioSource>
().mute = false;
```

```
            volumeSlider.enabled = true;
        }
    }
}
```

Congratulations! We now have a fully working and flexible template that we can use for navigating this and many other game projects, while handling different music tracks as well!

CHAPTER 7

"Jem Matcher:" Part 1

W ITH THE SCENE AND audio managers in place, we can now focus on the actual game and start working in the Game scene.

As noted in the previous chapter, the match-3 game we are going to build will be very basic; nonetheless, it will allow us to introduce a few new, very relevant concepts and programming techniques, while also reinforcing everything we have learned until now.

By default, "Jem Matcher" will be played on an 8×8 grid, with six different types of gems that will disappear whenever sequences of at least three gems of the same type are aligned next to each other, either horizontally or vertically. The game will allow for combos by shifting down remaining gems where underlying ones have been destroyed and filling up the resulting empty spaces with new random gems. The final objective will be to score the maximum possible number of points within 10 moves.

To start off, we need some nice gem graphics. Head to OpenGameArt. org to download some nice sprites (Figure 7.1) drawn by Ville Seppanen and provided under a Creative Commons license: http://opengameart.org/content/gem-jewel-diamond-glass.

Once the sprite sheet has been imported in Unity, we see that its dimensions are 512×512 and, since there are four gems per row, each individual sprite would ideally be seated in a cell of 128×128 pixels.

Make sure that the asset has been imported as "Sprite (2D and UI)," set "Sprite Mode" to "Multiple," otherwise we can't subdivide it in the Editor, and set "pixels per unit" to 128 so that each tile will occupy exactly 1 unit in our Game scene, as shown in Figure 7.2.

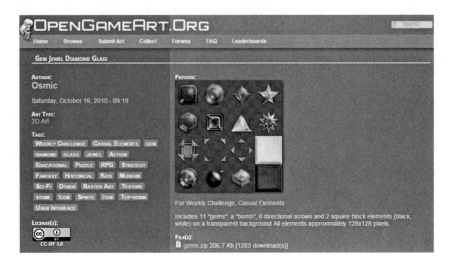

FIGURE 7.1   The graphics for our match-3 game.

FIGURE 7.2   The properties for the imported graphical assets.

Open the **Sprite Editor** and click on **Slice**. Automatic slicing won't work for us here (try it if you'd like to see what happens), so we need to choose **Grid by Cell Size** to manually set **Pixel Size** *x* and *y* to 128, as in Figure 7.3.

Notice now how the sprite sheet in the Assets shows each individual sprite with its own unique name (Figure 7.4).

With the graphics ready, we can start thinking about how to handle the actual game. First of all, we need to prepare a few prefabs, one for each gem type we want in the game. Six types seems like a good number, and we can pick gems 0, 1, 2, 3, 4, and 6 from Figure 7.4. To have all these prefabs ready, start by creating a new empty object in the scene; we can name

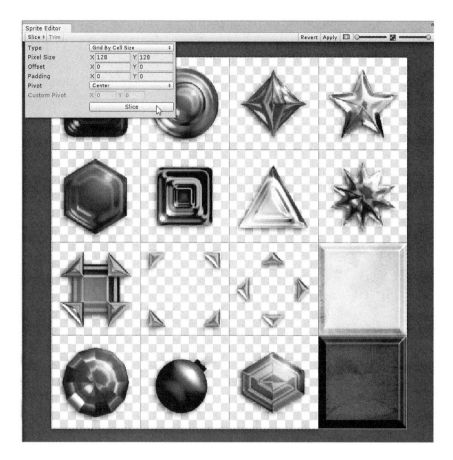

FIGURE 7.3   The sprite sheet sliced up in a 128 × 128 grid.

FIGURE 7.4   All sprites have been extracted from the original sprite sheet.

it **Gem Blue**, and add a **Sprite Renderer** component to it. In the Sprite field, pick the *gem2_0* sprite as shown in Figure 7.5, turn the object into a prefab by dragging it into our Assets/Prefab folder, and delete it from the scene. Each gem should also have its own ID and score value: add a very simple Script component to the prefab named **GemParameters**, where all we have to do is declare the following variables:

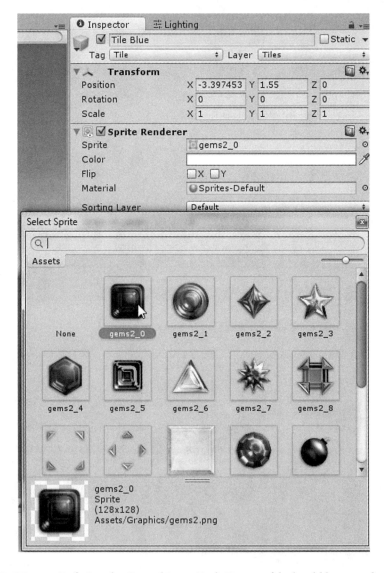

FIGURE 7.5   Defining the Gem objects. Each Gem prefab should be tagged with a "Tile" identifier so that we can easily reference them later.

```
public int id;
public int score;
```

We should also tag the prefab with a self-explanatory label, like "Gem" or "Tile," and, once done, we can use the **Ctrl+D** (or "Command+D" on a Mac) shortcut to duplicate the prefab and change its name and sprite to ultimately have all six different types of gems that we need. Number the IDs for each gem prefab progressively, starting from 0, and follow the same order as the sprites (i.e., blue gem should have ID equal to 0, green gem equal to 1, purple gem equal to 2, etc.). We will follow that order strictly from now on since, as we will better understand later, keeping it consistent throughout the game will actually allow us to simplify the overall checking of the grid and to know automatically which gem is occupying a specific tile.

However, feel free to set the score values for each gem in any way you see fit.

Last but not least, we also need to make a **tile selected** object to superimpose on a tile when the player clicks on it. Proceed as usual by using gem2_9 from Figure 7.4. We can turn this into a prefab as well, but we don't need to remove it from the scene: we will just need one instance of it to move around the scene as required.

Once all the new gem prefabs are ready, we need to think of the actual grid in which to place and manipulate them: as soon as the game starts, each cell in the grid has to be filled by a random tile, ready to be selected by the player. To handle the game logic, we should begin by creating another empty object; let's name it **GridManager**, and add a new C# script to it with the same name. This script will take care of initializing the grid, generating and destroying tiles, making them fall, swapping them when the player makes a legal move, and checking for eventual matches to trigger the aforementioned functionalities.

Open the script for editing, and let's declare the following variables:

```
public int [,] Grid;
public int GridWidth;
public int GridHeight;
public GameObject [] TilePrefabs;
```

These allow us to set up the bidimensional array that we will be using for the grid (whose dimensions we can then set in the Inspector, or even change later in the game if we ever want to have bigger or smaller grids for different levels) and an array of Game objects dedicated to the gem prefabs to be instantiated dynamically during the game.

The latter is particularly important and, like we just did for the prefab IDs, we should fill the array following the very same order as shown in Figure 7.6.

The Start() function will simply delegate two more methods to reset the grid and generate the first batch of random gems. We can call these two *ResetGrid()* and *GenerateGems()*, respectively:

```
void Start()  {
    ResetGrid();
    GenerateGems();
}
```

For the first, we can write the following code:

```
void ResetGrid()  {
    Grid = new int[GridWidth, GridHeight];
    for (int x = 0; x < GridWidth; x++) {
        for (int y = 0; y < GridHeight; y++) {
            Grid[x, y] = -1;
        }
    }
}
```

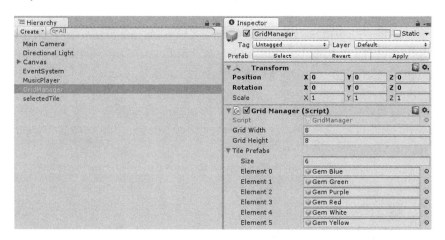

FIGURE 7.6   Initializing the GridManager object in the Inspector: the grid is going to be 8×8 tiles, and we are setting the Tile prefab array to have six elements. Note how Element 0 is the blue gem, to which we assigned an ID equal to 0 earlier; Element 1 is the green gem having an ID equal to 1, and so on. This will simplify some checking in the table later on.

What we do here is very straightforward: first, we define the 2D *Grid* array having the dimensions we decided, and then we scan the whole thing via two nested *for* loops, one for each dimension, to initialize all values to −1. In our game logic, a tile having the value of −1 means it is empty, while values from 0 to 5 will identify a specific gem using the convention established earlier.

The GenerateGems() method is also quite easy to follow:

```
public void GenerateGems() {
  for (int x = 0; x < GridWidth; x++) {
    for (int y = 0; y < GridHeight; y++) {
      if (Grid[x,y] == -1) // the cell is empty {
      int randomTile = Random.Range(0, TilePrefabs.
Length); Grid[x, y] = randomTile;
        Instantiate(TilePrefabs[randomTile],
new Vector2(x, y), Quaternion.identity);
        }
      }
    }
  }
}
```

Once again, we use two nested *for* loops to go through the array. Then, we check whether the tile under scrutiny is empty.* If so, we pick a random number between 0 and the length of the *TilePrefab* array (which we set to 6 in the Inspector earlier) to identify a specific tile and associate this value to the tile in the grid with current *x,y* coordinates.

Last, we actually *Instantiate* the selected gem in the Game scene at the very same *x,y* coordinates. Matching the coordinates of the object in the scene with the coordinates of its corresponding element in the 2D array is made possible by our scaling choices,† and it means that the first gem will be placed in (0,0) on the screen, with the others following accordingly. This trick will allow us to simplify our checks later on (otherwise, we would always remember to use some offset values when moving from the displayed grid to its logical representation in the array and vice versa), but it also means that we now need to reposition the camera so that the grid appears centered while we play. This isn't a big deal, obviously, so try to run the scene now: all

---

* Naturally, when calling this function the first time from Start(), all tiles will be empty, but doing this check will allow us to keep calling this very same function during the game and spawn new gems only in the places where previous ones have been destroyed.
† Remember that when we imported the gems graphics, we set *pixels per unit* to 128, while the sprite sheet had dimensions equal to 512 × 512 and included four gems per row. Each gem, then, being 128 × 128, will cover exactly 1 unit in Unity on each dimension.

the gems should be instantiated and displayed in the Game space, so we can simply move the camera via the Inspector to find its optimal position and then actually shift the camera there once back in editing mode.*

While we can't interact with the gems yet, it is actually a good time to start discussing the game logic we will need to swap them, to check for matches, and, eventually, to destroy the matched ones.

Swapping gems is another simple task that we can easily accomplish with the following method:

```
public void SwapGems(GameObject gem1, GameObject
gem2)  {
  Vector2 temp = gem1.transform.position;

  // move the actual tiles
  gem1.transform.position = gem2.transform.position;
  gem2.transform.position = temp;

  // change the values in the underlying grid
accordingly
  Grid[(int)gem1.transform.position.x,(int)gem1.
transform.position.y] = gem1.GetComponent<Gem
Parameters>().id;
  Grid[(int)gem2.transform.position.x,(int)gem2.
transform.position.y] = gem2.GetComponent<GemParamet
ers>().id;
  }
```

Here, we receive the gems we want to swap in our move as parameters and use a temp variable of type Vector2 to store the coordinates of one gem while swapping them. After this, each gem will appear in its newly assigned tile; but this is not enough, as we also have to update the corresponding representation of the underlying grid. We do this in the following two lines of code, by assigning the gem's ID (stored in the **GemParameters** script component for each gem) to the corresponding Grid element.

Checking for matching gems is a little more articulated, and it is something that we can do in different ways. A very straightforward way is to check for three or more matches across all the rows first, then checking across the columns and acting accordingly.

---

* An easy way to automatically move the game camera to match the view in the editing scene is to use the 'GamObject/Align with View' menu command after having selected the camera in the Hierarchy.

The *CheckMatches()* method will be called after every move made by the player and will return true if matches have been found, or false otherwise. We can start it by declaring variables for tracking how many matches have been found across rows and columns, plus a counter that we will use while scanning the grid to keep track of how many equal gems, one after the other, we have found so far:

```
public bool CheckMatches()  {
  int counter;
  int matchesC = 0; // how many matches on the columns
  int matchesR = 0; // how many matches on the rows
```

The actual scan follows, where for each row, we first reset the *counter* variable to 1, and then we check across the column whether the next element stored in the Grid array is the same as the current one, assuming both are not empty (i.e., equal to –1). If so, we increment counter until we find a different value or the row ends. When this happens, we can simply check if counter reached a value of at least 3 to determine whether we had a match, in which case we will call a yet-to-be-written method, *DestroyGems*, by specifying the (*x,y*) location in the grid of the last matching element, how long the matching sequence is, and whether the match is across a row or a column (encoding the latter parameter as a Boolean variable):

```
 // scanning columns
  for (int x = 0; x < GridWidth; x++) {
   counter = 1;
   for (int y = 0; y < GridHeight-1; y++)  {
   if (Grid[x,y] == Grid[x, y+1] && Grid[x,y] != 1) {
                counter++;
         }
    else // next tile is different, let's check if we
had a match
        {
          if (counter >= 3 )  {
               matchesC++;
             // call function to destroy tiles
             DestroyGems(x,y,counter, false);
          }
          //reset counter and keep searching
          counter = 1;
```

```
        }
    // special case: we have a match but the row is over
    if (counter >=3 && y+1 == GridHeight-1)  {
          matchesC++;
          DestroyGems(x,y+1,counter, false);
        }
      }
    }
```

Scanning rows for possible matches follows exactly the same procedure but with *x* and *y* variables reversed:

```
// scanning rows
for (int y = 0; y < GridHeight; y++) {
     counter = 1;
     for (int x = 0; x < GridWidth-1; x++) {
     if (Grid[x,y] == Grid[x+1, y] && Grid[x,y] != 1) {
        counter++;
       }
      else  {
      if (counter >= 3 ) {
           matchesR++;
           // call function to destroy tiles
           DestroyGems(x,y,counter, true);
         }
         //reset counter and keep searching
         counter = 1;
       }
     // special case: we have a match but the row is
     over
     if (counter >=3 && x+1 == GridWidth-1)  {
           matchesR++;
          DestroyGems(x+1,y,counter, true);
         }
       }
     }
```

Following this, we can end the method by calling

```
    return (matchesC > 0 || matchesR > 0) ? true :
false;
}
```

where we return either *true* or *false* according to either value of *matchesC* or *matchesR*. Notice how, to return the Boolean value, we use the so-called **ternary operator**, whose syntax requires a condition between parentheses followed by a question mark and a statement that is executed in case the condition is true. Last, this is also followed by a colon and the statement to be executed if the condition was false. This is a very handy operator common across C-type languages that can help us to compact our code when needed. In our specific case, we can read the instruction as "*If either matchesC or matchesR is greater than 0 return true, otherwise return false.*"

With CheckMatches() done, we can discuss the other method that we were calling from there, that is, DestroyGems. As we said, this will take a a few parameters: the (*x,y*) coordinate of the last matched gem in the grid, a counter indicating how long the matching sequence is, and a Boolean identifying whether the match is on a row or a column.

The idea here is to retrieve all the Game objects corresponding to those matching grid coordinates, that is, the gems, starting from the last one, which we found by scanning all gems across columns or rows while looking at their position on the game space.*

Once found, we destroy it and go back as far as stated by the counter variable, destroying each gem that made up the match while also clearing the grid element by resetting it to −1. In the following code snippet, this is done for both rows and columns.

```
void DestroyGems(int x, int y, int counter, bool row)
{ // let's start from gem at (x,y) and destroy counter
elements backwards
  GameObject[] GemsToDestroy;
  // remember all gems are tagged as "Tile"
  GemsToDestroy = GameObject.
FindGameObjectsWithTag("Tile");
  // scan either columns or rows till we get into
position
  foreach (GameObject t in GemsToDestroy)
  {
          if (row == false)      {
    for (int i = 0; i < counter; i++) if (t.transform.
position.x == x && t.transform.position.y == (y-i))   {
          Destroy(t);
```

---

* Remember, gems have been placed so that their position (*x,y*) in Unity units is the same as their (*x,y*) representation in the grid.

```
      Grid[x,y-i] = -1; // grid reset
      }
    }
// match is on a row. Same thing.
  else {
          for (int i = 0; i < counter; i++)
          if (t.transform.position.x == (x-i) && t.
transform.position.y == y)  {
                    Destroy(t);
                    Grid[x-i,y] = -1;
              }
          }
        }
      }
    }
```

Having destroyed the matched gems and cleared the underlying 2D Grid array, we now have some holes in the grid that we should fill by having the gems above those empty slots fall down. To do this, we can proceed in a similar way to what we just did: we make an array including all gems,

```
public void FallingGems()   {
  int counter;
  GameObject[] Tiles;
  Tiles = GameObject.FindGameObjectsWithTag("Tile");
```

and then we scan the grid across its columns starting from the bottom (i.e., (0,0)) to look for empty tiles and gems above them. We use a variable named counter to keep track of how many tiles we need to move down: every time we find an empty tile in the grid, we increment counter by 1.

```
  for (int x = 0; x < GridWidth; x++) {
        counter = 0;
        for (int  y = 0; y < GridHeight; y++) {
        if (Grid[x,y] == -1)  {
        counter++; // how many cells shall we shift
the tile?
        }
```

If, instead, the tile under analysis is not empty, we check counter to see if this needs to be shifted down, that is, we counted some empty space below it. If so, we update the corresponding grid values, resetting the one on top to −1.

```
else if (counter > 0) {
  // update the grid
  Grid[x,y-counter] = Grid[x,y] ;
  Grid[x,y] = -1;
```

Last, we also shift down the actual gem Game object to its new place.

```
foreach (GameObject t in Tiles) {
    if (t.transform.position.x == x && t.transform.
position.y == y)  {
    t.transform.position = new Vector2 (x, t.
transform.position.y - counter);
        }
      }
   }
   }
 }
 }
```

All the essential logic to make the matching gameplay is there now, but we can't play the game until we actually let the player select a gem and move it.

In Figure 7.4, besides all the gems, we also selected a sprite to work as a gem selector. Make a new object with a Sprite Renderer component using such a sprite, name it **SelectedGem**, and bring it into the scene but outside the visible area of the game, ready to be moved whenever needed (Figure 7.7).

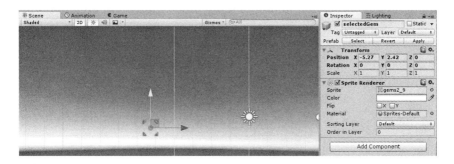

FIGURE 7.7   The SelectedGem object placed outside the camera view, ready to jump in whenever needed.

To select a gem, we will simply click on it via the mouse. This sounds very simple, but it isn't as straightforward as we may think as we have to move from the 2D (*x,y*) mouse coordinates to pick an underlying object in the actual scene coordinates. To achieve this, Unity provides us with a very flexible *Ray* structure. In a nutshell, rays are infinite lines starting at an origin and going in some direction, enabling us to intercept colliders belonging to an object in their path. To select a gem, then, what we will be doing is shooting a ray from the current mouse position downward, followed by the *GetRayIntersection* method to check if the ray actually hit anything. This method belongs to the *Physics2D* class and takes as parameters the ray itself, the maximum *distance* the ray should travel, and a specific *layer* that we may want to check the collision in.

Layers are another important concept that we should get accustomed to, and we can easily assign an object to a layer via the Inspector. In our very simple game, with only one set of objects all in the same plane, layers are not really necessary, but let's use them anyway to understand how they work, since they would be fundamental in more complex scenarios where we have overlapping objects and we only want to hit specific ones and go through the others.

As shown in Figure 7.8, add a new layer named "Tiles" and select it for every gem prefab.

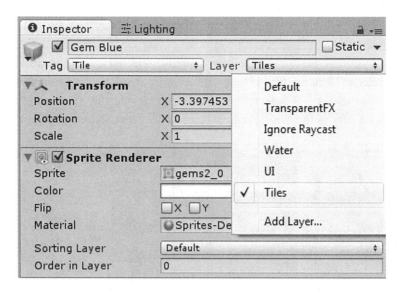

FIGURE 7.8   All Gem prefabs should belong to a layer named Tiles. Raycasts will only hit colliders belonging to objects within this specific layer. Adding new layers works exactly like adding new tags.

For rays to actually hit objects, we also need to add a *Box Collider 2D* to all gems prefabs; once done with this step, we are finally ready to start coding. Add a new script component to *GridManager* and call it **PlayerSelect**. Open it in the editor and start adding the following variables:

```
public class PlayerSelect : MonoBehaviour {
  private GridManager gridManager;
  // selector sprite we use to highlight the selected
tile
  public GameObject selector;
  // layer to check for raycasts targets.
  public LayerMask tileLayer;
  // gem selected
  private GameObject activeGem;
  // tile to move to. Must be a neighbour of
activeGem
  private GameObject destinationTile;
```

So far, we have defined references to the GridManager script (to access its methods later when needed), to the selected gem sprite, to the layer we want to target with our ray casts, to the gem we want to select, and, finally, to the specific tile in the grid where we want to move it. According to the basic set of rules we decided at the beginning of the chapter, we also want to add another couple of variables to track eventual combos and the amount of moves left, eventually leading us to the Game Over script where we may want to check for a high score.

```
  // keeping track of combos
  private int combos;
  // moves left
  private int movesLeft;
```

Following this, we should set *tileLayer* and *selector* from the *Inspector* while, in *Start()*, we can simply retrieve the GridManager component and initialize *combos* to 0 and *movesLeft* to 10:

```
void Start() {
    // retrieve the Grid Manager component
    gridManager = GetComponent<GridManager>();
    combos = 0;
    movesLeft = 10;
  }
```

In *Update()*, we check for a left mouse click via the *Input.GetKeyDown* method. If we have no active gem selected, we call a method to select it, whereas if we had one already, it means we just clicked on the destination tile we want to move it to, so we call a different method to execute the gem swapping:

```
void Update()  {
   // left mouse click
   if (Input.GetKeyDown(KeyCode.Mouse0)) {
     if (activeGem == null)
       SelectGem();
     else
       AttemptMove();
   }
}
```

It is in *SelectGem()* that we finally shoot the ray by using the *ScreenPointToRay* method of the camera class, specifying the current mouse position as its parameter. Checking for a collision happens right after it by calling the GetRayIntersection method and specifying the ray we just shot, a distance to cover (our camera has a *z* coordinate of −10 while the plane where we are placing the gems has *z* equal to 0, so anything greater than 10 will be enough), plus an eventual layer to check (referenced by the tileLayer variable). If we hit a gem in the specified layer, we associate it with the *activeGem* object by retrieving the specific gem Game object from the collider we hit, and then we move the selector to the gem in the very same position so that we can highlight it in the board.

```
void SelectGem() {
Ray ray = Camera.main.ScreenPointToRay(Input.
mousePosition);
RaycastHit2D hit = Physics2D.
GetRayIntersection(ray,50f,tileLayer);
  if (hit) {
     activeGem = hit.collider.gameObject;
     selector.transform.position = activeGem.transform.
position;
   }
}
```

If, instead, we already had a gem selected (i.e., activeGem is not null), it means that we are clicking on a different one to swap them. In this case, from *Update()* we call *AttemptMove()* instead, where we repeat the ray shooting procedure to select the other gem.*

Assuming we have a hit, we update *destinationTile* with the hit object and perform a check, via a dedicated function, to be sure that the gem we want to swap is a neighbor of the first one. If it is, we reset the combos counter and decrease movesLeft by 1 before accessing the *SwapGems* method in GridManager and calling another method, *ApplyMove()*, to complete the process by checking for matches in the grid.

However, if the neighbor check fails, it means that we are clicking on another tile somewhere else on the board to move that one instead. Hence, we restart the process by calling SelectGem() once more.

The last possible case we have to consider here is if the hit misses, that is, the player is clicking in some other part of the screen. In this case, we will call another method, *ResetActive()*, that takes care of resetting activeGem and moving the selector out of the screen.

```
void AttemptMove() {
    Ray ray = Camera.main.ScreenPointToRay(Input.
mousePosition);
    RaycastHit2D hit = Physics2D.
GetRayIntersection(ray, 50f, tileLayer);
    if (hit)   {
        destinationTile = hit.collider.gameObject;
        if (NeighborCheck(destinationTile)) {
        // reset the combo counter and update moves
left.
        combos = 0;
        movesLeft--;
        // we need to switch the two tiles
        gridManager.SwapGems(activeGem, destinationTile);
        ApplyMove();
        }
        else // if we are clicking a different gem which
is not a neighbour, we select this one instead
        {
```

* Since we are reusing the same lines of code more than once, we should actually write a dedicated *Shoot()* method to return the hit *RayCast2D* to both *SelectGem()* and *AttemptMove()*. The corresponding code in the Unity package for this project actually does this, but here I preferred to simply rewrite the code for clarity instead of breaking it further with another method.

```
        SelectGem();
      }
    }
  else // if we are clicking outside the board and
hit fails       {
      ResetActive();
    }
  }

  void ResetActive()  {
    activeGem = null;
    selector.transform.position = new Vector2(-10f, 0f);
  }
```

To check neighbors in *NeighborCheck()*, we can simply compare the *x* and *y* positions of the two gems and, if their combined difference is 1 (meaning they are on the same row or column but adjacent to each other), we can confirm they are actually neighbors.

```
bool NeighborCheck(GameObject objectToCheck)  {
    // either same column and next/previous row or
same row and next/previous column
    // we need to cast from float to int
    int xDifference = Mathf.Abs((int)activeGem.
transform.position.x - (int)objectToCheck.transform.
position.x);
    int yDifference = Mathf.Abs((int)activeGem.
transform.position.y - (int)objectToCheck.transform.
position.y);
    if (xDifference + yDifference == 1 {
      return true;
    }
    else {
      return false;
    }
  }
```

Finally, ApplyMove() is where we actually perform the swap, as long as the previously discussed CheckMatches() returns true. If so, and the corresponding gems were destroyed with their underlying tiles cleared, we call additional methods in GridManager to have any eventual gem sitting above the now empty slots moved down. This is followed by a call to fill those tiles once again with new, random gems. We should also increase the combos counter (e.g., we may want to use this later and implement a score multiplier if players manage to score a certain number of combos) and call ApplyMove() recursively to actually check whether the newly generated gems could trigger new matches, that is, combos!

The combos variable is also used to check the case when the proposed move doesn't actually trigger any match. What we should do in this case depends on the rules that we want to apply to the game. Should such a move be allowed? Most match-3 games don't, so we can also decide to revert the move by reswapping the two gems and increasing the movesLeft counter before also resetting the active gem and tile by calling ResetActive().

```
void ApplyMove() {
    // we need to check matches. If not, we need to
return the tiles to their original position OR remove
a player move/life
    bool match = gridManager.CheckMatches();
    // if we had a match and destroyed some tiles, we
need to traslate and repopulate the missing cells in
the grid with new tiles
    if (match) {
        // let's shift the tiles!
        gridManager.FallingGems();
        // and repopulate the grid, if we like
        gridManager.GenerateGems();
        // if we chose to repopulate the grid, we'd
check for combos so we keep track of matches found and
use recursion to find more in the newly spawned gems.
        combos++;
        ApplyMove();
    }
    else if (combos == 0) // move didn't trigger any
match: unless we allow generic tile swapping, we have
to cancel this:
    {
        gridManager.SwapGems(destinationTile,
activeGem); // re-swapping the non matching tiles
        movesLeft++; // restore the move counter
    }
```

```
    // either way, we can now remove the highlight
cursor
    ResetActive();
  }
}
```

We can start playing the game now, as we should be able to actually swap, match, and destroy the gems!

We covered a lot of ground and coded quite a bit as well in this chapter. To actually consolidate what we have learned so far, it is of paramount importance that you don't limit yourself to copying, testing, and understanding the code proposed but you also take an extra step and do some additional modifications or even refactor some parts of it to improve and polish what we started. For example, you may try the following exercises before proceeding further.

EXERCISE 1

Add a flag in the Options screen to specify whether or not we want new gems to be generated to replace those that have been matched and removed from the board. This will change the game drastically (i.e., the objective now becomes trying to clear the board), but both gameplay modes are actually quite fun and are used in a variety of match-3 games.

EXERCISE 2

You may have noticed that our matching algorithm only finds matches on individual rows and columns and can't identify cross or t-shaped matches, since a gem belonging to two matching configurations will be destroyed as soon as the first match has been found, breaking the later match. This is an important feature that we are missing, and it is something we definitely want to add in a proper game. Your task then is to modify the game, enabling it to correctly identify those patterns as well.

HINT: A possible way of doing this is to first add a "selected" flag to each tile and then, when checking rows and columns for matches in CheckMatches(), we don't destroy matched gems right away but simply use the flag to identify them. Once all rows and columns have been checked, we can call DestroyTiles(), where we simply scan the grid again and destroy all marked tiles at once.

CHAPTER 8

"Jem Matcher:" Part 2

D O YOU REMEMBER THAT we also attached a script named *GemParameters* to every Gem prefab, earlier on? In it, we defined not only the gem *ID* but also its *score* value, so it is a good time now to actually use those scores and show them on-screen after each move.

In each move, when we check for matches, every destroyed gem will contribute to the score by adding its own value. We can also use the number of matches found to define a combo variable for a multiplier effect.

Let's start by adding the relevant Text objects in the Canvas: two to use as labels, and two to actually display the moves left and score numbers. Once done, the empty playfield of the *Game* scene should look similar to Figure 8.1.

We can now think about implementing the moves counter and the score system. The former is quite straightforward and requires only some simple additions in the *PlayerSelect* script, starting from the declaration of a new public text field to connect to the number displayed on the Canvas.

Remember that accessing any user interface (UI) element requires first adding the following line at the beginning of the script,

```
using UnityEngine.UI;
```

and then we can add an appropriate variable in the class declaration:

```
public Text txtMoves;
```

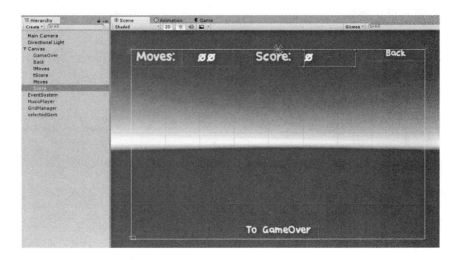

FIGURE 8.1   Adding movesLeft and Score fields to the Canvas of the Game scene.

Once we drag and drop the *Moves* text field from the Hierarchy to the PlayerSelect component of the *GridManager* object in the Inspector, we are ready to start accessing and changing it from our script.

The PlayerSelect script already has a *movesLeft* variable that we defined previously: this is initialized to 10 in *Start()*; it gets decremented in *AttemptMove()* and, eventually, restored in *ApplyMove()*, if the move was illegal.

All we have to do is to define a new method that we can call whenever needed, that is, at the end of Start() to initialize the field with its starting value, and at the end of ApplyMove(). We can call this method *UpdateMovesTxt()*, and the line we need will simply assign the movesLeft value (converted to String) to the text property of the *txtMoves* Text object:

```
txtMoves.text = movesLeft.ToString();
```

We may also take care of the Game Over case here, that is, when the movesLeft counter reaches 0. We could simply load the Game Over scene directly, but, to be consistent with the overall framework we established, we should get a reference to the *GameManager* object and use its methods instead.

The method will then look like this:

```
void UpdateMovesTxt() {
  // display moves left
  txtMoves.text = movesLeft.ToString();
  // if moves = 0, game over!
  if (movesLeft == 0) {
    // retrieve the game manager object
    GameObject manager;
    manager = GameObject.Find("GameManager");
    manager.GetComponent<GameManager>().
    LoadSceneByName("03 GameOver");
  }
}
```

Handling the score is a bit more complicated, but it also gives us the opportunity to introduce a new feature: *PlayerPrefs*. "Player Preferences" is a Unity class that allows us to store values between player sessions and to share them easily among different scenes and objects within the game. Essentially, it gives us an easy way to define and use variables that we can store and retrieve whenever needed.

Each item in PlayerPrefs is made by two parts: a *key*, which is a string identifying its name, and its actual *value*, which can be an Int, Float, or String. Setting and getting values back is done by calling the corresponding methods, and the class also provides methods to check whether a key exists already, to save all keys and values locally on the player's device (regardless of what is being used, i.e., PC, smartphone, etc.), and to delete one record or all records.

In our case, we will need to access and manipulate the player's scores across a few methods in both PlayerSelect and GridManager scripts and, possibly, even to save them to disk if we ever decide to implement a leaderboard, for example. Using PlayerPrefs can definitely make our life easier.*

The Start() function in PlayerSelect is where we can declare our score-related key. We need one for the score itself; one for the score obtained in the last move, *lastmovescore* (since we want to multiply it by the combos variable); and one for a *highscore*. Setting the first two is very straightforward:

```
PlayerPrefs.SetInt("lastmovescore",0);
PlayerPrefs.SetInt("score",0);
```

---

* A warning note, though: setting keys in PlayerPrefs is like having global variables that can be accessed and manipulated by anything in the game, any time. This may look very handy at first, but, as all experienced programmers know, it can also be a serious liability in big projects, as it may be difficult to track down where a change happened, making any debugging much more difficult.

However, for highscore, we should first do a check to see whether the key already exists and initialize it only if it doesn't, that is, if it is the first time the game is being played. This can be easily achieved by checking the *HasKey* property of PlayerPrefs for the desired key.

```
if (!PlayerPrefs.HasKey("highscore")) {
    PlayerPrefs.SetInt("highscore",0);
}
```

How and where shall we now compute the score?

First, whenever the player tries a new move (which we check for in AttemptMove()), we need to reset lastmovescore in PlayerPrefs:*

```
PlayerPrefs.SetInt("lastmovescore", 0);
```

AttemptMove() then calls ApplyMove(), which checks if there is any match and destroys the corresponding gems via the appropriate methods in GridManager. It is, in fact, *DestroyGems()* that takes care of eliminating any gem belonging to a recognized match, so it is there that we should update the score.

We should then modify DestroyGems() to first retrieve lastmovescore from PlayerPrefs and save its value in a local variable, and then, right before destroying a gem, we increment the local variable with the score assigned to the gem itself.

Once all the matching gems have been destroyed, we can update the original lastmovescore variable.

The updated DestroyGems method will then look like the following (new lines are in bold):

```
void DestroyGems(int x, int y, int counter, bool row)  {
    GameObject[] GemsToDestroy;
    GemsToDestroy = GameObject.FindGameObjectsWithTag
    ("Tile");
    // we need to retrieve lastmovescore from PlayerPrefs
    int lastscore = PlayerPrefs.GetInt("lastmovescore");
    foreach (GameObject t in GemsToDestroy)
    {
    if (row == false)
```

* Insert this line before calling GridManager.SwapGems().

```
{
  for (int i = 0; i < counter; i++)
  if (t.transform.position.x == x && t.transform.
  position.y == (y-i))
  {
    // compute score from the destroyed gems
    lastscore += t.GetComponent<GemParameters>().
    score;

    Destroy(t);
    Grid[x,y-i] = -1; // the grid position is now
    empty
  }
} else {
    for (int i = 0; i < counter; i++)
    if (t.transform.position.x == (x-i) &&
t.transform.position.y == y)
      {
      // compute score from the destroyed gems
      lastscore += t.GetComponent<GemParameters>().
      score;

      Destroy(t);
      Grid[x-i,y] = -1;
        }
      }
    }
    // update score done in the last move
  PlayerPrefs.SetInt("lastmovescore", lastscore);
}
```

Once all matches in the current grid have been taken care of, the program goes back to ApplyMove(), where the grid is updated by shifting gems down and generating new ones. Here is where we should actually update the score on display, right before calling ApplyMove() again to check for any additional, new match. For this purpose, we can declare a new method called *UpdateScore()*, having in input one parameter of type *int* to pass the combos variable.

This method first retrieves the previous total score and the current value obtained in the last (possibly still ongoing) move, multiplies the latter by the *combos* parameter for extra bonus points, and then adds these to the total. Last, it needs to update the corresponding variables in PlayerPrefs by resetting lastmovescore (in case there is an additional combo with the newly spawned gems), updating the score as well as updating the corresponding text field in the UI:

```
void UpdateScore(int combos)  {
    // retrieve score from
    int score = PlayerPrefs.GetInt("score");
    // retrieve last move score
    int lastmove = PlayerPrefs.GetInt("lastmovescore");
   // multiply by combos? Bonus points for combos
    lastmove *= combos;
    score += lastmove;
    // reset move score for next combo, if any
    PlayerPrefs.SetInt("lastmovescore", 0);
    // update values
    PlayerPrefs.SetInt("score", score);
    // display new value
    txtScore.text = score.ToString();
  }
}
```

Play the game again, and check that everything works as expected. The implementation of the highscore shouldn't present any problem now, and we leave it out as a possible exercise at the end of the chapter. On the other hand, wouldn't it be nice if we had some simple explosion effect when a gem is destroyed? So far, gems get moved, destroyed, and replaced, but there is no visual feedback. Having at least a few basic but colorful particles would definitely increase the appeal of the prototype.

In the Game scene, add a new *Particle System* object, either from the *Game Object* menu or from the *Create* drop-down list in the *Hierarchy*. In the Inspector, we will now have all the parameters of the object to start designing the visual effect, neatly divided into modules (Figure 8.2).

Reset the particles' *Transform* position, if needed, and zoom on them (by selecting it in the Hierarchy and then pressing F while the mouse cursor is in the scene window). Let's say we want our particles to act like a short, fast, 360° burst, with colors ranging from yellow to red. For simplicity's sake, we can use the default particle texture, but naturally, if you would like to import a new image and design things differently, feel free to do so. To simulate a short burst, let's first reduce the duration to 1.00 and have Start Lifetime and Speed reduced to 1. On one hand, these changes

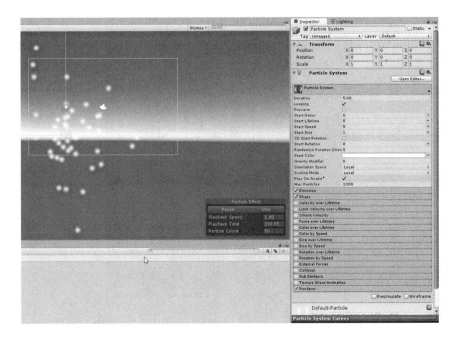

FIGURE 8.2   The new particle system in the scene with all its parameters.*

will make the particles disappear faster and stay close to the origin. On the other hand, we can make them bigger, so we can increase their size to 5, turning them into a sort of cloud. Since we want this to be a short burst, we should also uncheck the *Looping* flag, but for now, we can leave it on to see the effect of our changes in real time in the scene. For the colors, choose **Random between two colors** in the *Start Color* dropdown, and then pick a bright red and a bright yellow. Last, the shape. Expand the corresponding module and select Circle, with a radius of 1 and an arc of 360°. The Inspector will then look like Figure 8.3, while the effect looks like Figure 8.4.

What we have to do now is rename the particles effect something a little more descriptive, like "Explosion," for example; turn it into a prefab; and remove the original one from the Game scene. An instance of the particles, in fact, will be added to the scene whenever we destroy a gem. Since we are destroying the gems in the GridManager script of the GridManager object, we should also take care of the particles there.

---

* A detailed explanation of each parameter can be found in the official Unity manual under the Particle System Reference section.

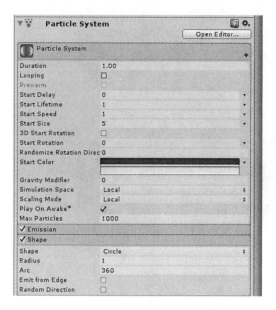

FIGURE 8.3   The final parameters for the new particles. Remember to deselect the Looping flag once satisfied with the resulting effect, and then check the actual burst by pressing Stop and then Simulate on the small window that appears in the scene once the Particle object is selected. Leave "Play on Awake" selected, so that the effect will play as soon as it is instantiated in the scene.

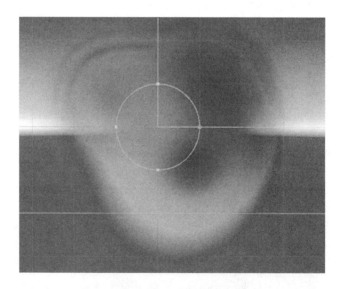

FIGURE 8.4   The resulting explosion effect.

Hence, open GridManager and start by declaring a new public variable of type ParticleSystem, which we will use to reference the object:

```
public ParticleSystem explosion;
```

Then, at the bottom of the script, we write a new method to instantiate the particles. We can call this *Explode()* and define it to have two parameters in input, identifying the coordinates where the particles should appear.

```
// instantiate explosion effect
void Explode(float x, float y) {
  Instantiate(explosion, new Vector3 (x,y,0f),
  Quaternion.identity);
  }
```

We can then call this method from the DestroyGems() function, right before calling *Destroy(t)* (where *t* is the matched gem we are destroying) when scanning the rows and columns:

```
Explode (t.transform.position.x, t.transform.
position.y);
```

The explosions we are creating will not destroy themselves, though: they will play only once (since we previously unchecked the **Loop** flag), but they will still remain in the scene. To actually remove them and free the corresponding memory, we should also add a very simple script to the *ParticleSystem* prefab. Call this *ExplosionScript*, and then add a line in its *Update()* method, where we go to check whether the ParticleSystem component of the object is still playing. If not, it's time to destroy the object itself.

```
void Update () {
if (this.gameObject.GetComponent<ParticleSystem>().
isPlaying == false)
   Destroy(this.gameObject);
  }
```

Play the game once again and see the explosions appearing (and disappearing from the Hierarchy, once done) whenever we match tiles, including for any eventual combos that happen with newly spawned gems!

In this chapter, we added some important features to the game and, in doing so, we introduced PlayerPrefs, to save and retrieve values across scripts, scenes, and playing sessions and *Particles*. Unity provides a very flexible and powerful editing system for the latter. The best (and only) way to actually master it is experimenting with it to see how changing each parameter's value would affect the resulting effect. Have fun with particles!

EXERCISE

We defined a highscore key in PlayerPrefs, but we didn't implement that feature yet. Complete the task by updating the highscore value in the Game Over scene, and then have it also displayed during the game as another UI element. Also, display the player's score in the Game Over scene, together with a congratulation message when a high score has been achieved.

CHAPTER 9

Moving to Mobile

W ITH "JEM MATCHER" WORKING on PC, we can finally set up the environment to deploy it on an Android-based mobile device.

First of all, we need to install the Android Software Development Kit (SDK) found at https://developer.android.com/sdk/index.html#Other (you may install the whole Android Studio suite if you prefer, but it won't actually be necessary if we plan on developing Android games by only using Unity). Look for "SDK Tools Only" for your Windows or OSX-based computer and download it. The next step is to download the Java Development Kit (JDK) from http://www.oracle.com/technetwork/java/javase/downloads/index.html. Pick up the latest version for your specific operating system (OS). Note that there are both 32 and 64 bit downloads: if you can't find out what your central processing unit (CPU) architecture is, you may download the 32 bit version (x86), which will work on either.

Once the JDK has been downloaded and installed, we can proceed to install the Android SDK, which will require a little bit more attention. First of all, write down the destination folder path that you are install-ing the SDK into (we will have to paste it in Unity later), then, once the SDK installation is over, we will need to launch the "SDK Manager" we find within the "Android SDK Tools" folder in the Start menu. The SDK Manager will look similar to Figure 9.1.

For simplicity, let's click on **Deselect all** first, and then proceed by check-ing the latest versions of *Android SDK Tools*, *Android SDK Platforms-tools*, and *Android SDK Build-tools* under the **Tools** folder, followed by the **SDK Platform** items in the folders of the corresponding Android version that we want to support and test our game on.

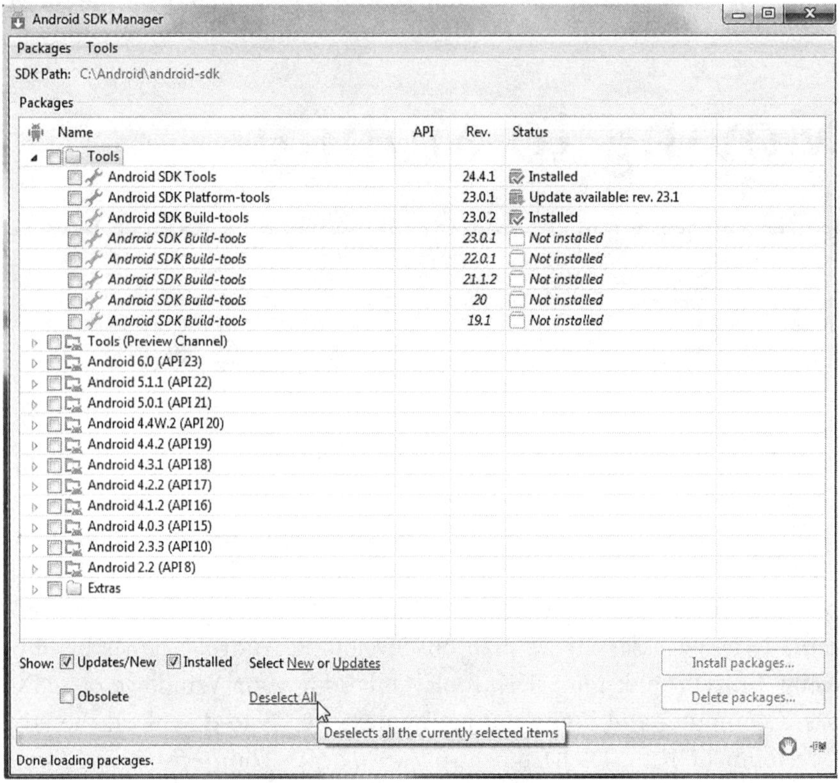

FIGURE 9.1   Downloading additional components from the SDK Manager.

Click on Install, accept the licenses, and proceed.*

Once everything is done, we can close the SDK Manager and turn our attention to the phone we want to test the game on. To do so, on our Android device, we need to activate the so-called **Developer Mode**: go to *Settings* and look for something like **About Phone** or **About Device**. Get into that submenu, and look for **Build Number**:† keep tapping it until you get a "developer mode enabled" message, after which a new menu named "Developer Options" will appear in the "About Phone" screen. Many new options will be included in this section, which will become accessible as soon as we actually turn the whole menu on by pressing a simple switch on the top right corner of the screen. Find **USB Debugging** and check it.

---

* If anything goes wrong or you have any doubts, you may check the official documentation at http://developer.android.com/sdk/installing/adding-packages.html.
† In some Android versions, this is further hidden into a "Software Info" submenu.

The phone should now be ready to receive the game from Unity for testing purposes.

Back in Unity, open the "Build Settings" menu and click on Android and then on the **Switch Platform** button (Figure 9.2). Unity will then optimize and convert certain assets included in the project (like audio files) according to the new platform's requirements.

Once it's done, click on **Player Settings**: it is here that we find all the options we need to change the **Product Name**, add icons (if we don't specify any, the default Unity logo will be used), allow portrait/landscape orientation, and much more.

At this stage, we also need to define the so-called **Bundle Identifier**, which we will need in any marketplace to uniquely identify our game. This is found in the **Other Settings** module (Figure 9.3), where we also find

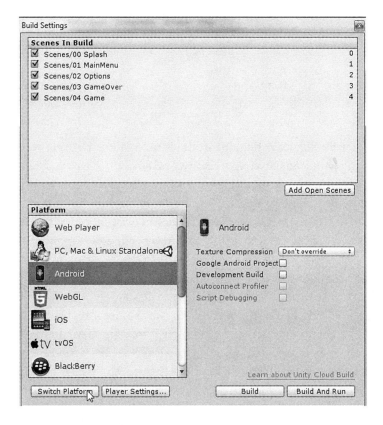

FIGURE 9.2 Simply selecting a new target platform isn't enough to actually activate it: we also need to explicitly switch to it by pressing the corresponding button.

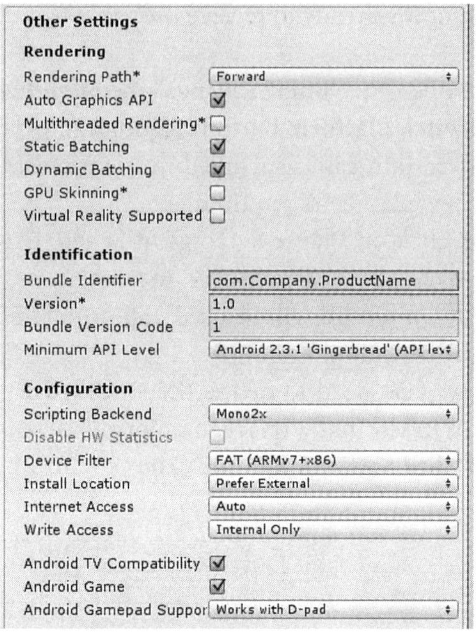

FIGURE 9.3   The Bundle Identifier is in the "Other Settings." It should be written in a reverse domain-like form, that is, "com.YourCompany.YourGame."

options for forcing a particular install location, allowing Internet access, supporting gamepads or virtual reality, and so on.

The **Publishing Settings** (Figure 9.4) are also very important; in fact, to actually distribute games, these have to be signed with a specific key unique to us. Here, Unity allows us to select an existing key or create a new one by selecting the corresponding checkbox before clicking the "Browse Keystore" button, which will now be used to create a new file instead of selecting an existing one.

When browsing for a location to save the new keystore, its default name will be something like **user.keystore**, but we should probably personalize it with our company's name, for example. Once the keystore name and location have been decided, we have to click the *Alias* drop-down menu and choose the option **Create a new key** (Figure 9.5), which will, in turn, open up a new window (Figure 9.6) where we can specify its alias, password, and other details.

Note that, for security reasons, Unity won't store the password together with the other project settings, so we will have to input it every time we need to sign a new build for distribution (i.e., don't forget it!).

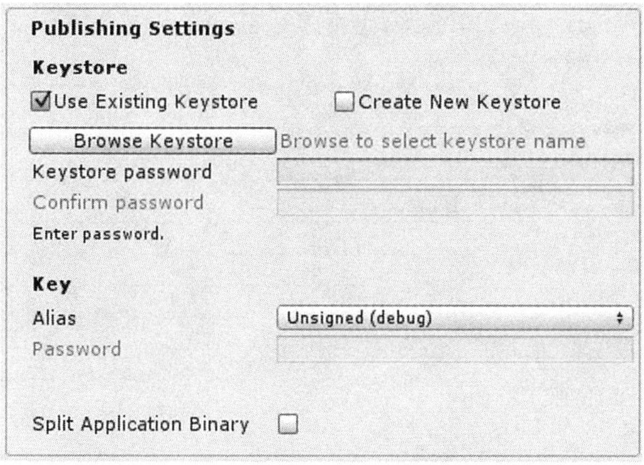

FIGURE 9.4   Before distributing a game, we need to sign it with a key. We can use an existing one (providing its password) or create a new one directly from Unity.

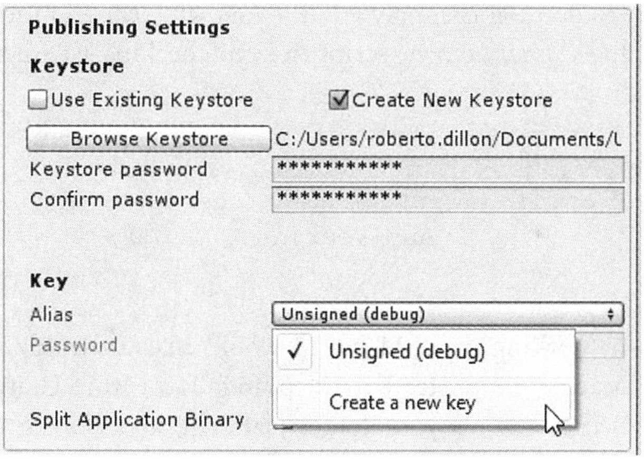

FIGURE 9.5   Once a new keystore name and location have been decided, we can proceed to create the actual key.

Try building the game and testing it on your device: Unity's buttons and Input class are smart enough to automatically translate mouse clicks into touch events so that the game will actually be playable without issues. The *Quit* button in the *Main Menu* scene also works properly and closes the game. On the other hand, pressing the *Back* button on the device won't have any effect.

To fix this, we have to know that, by default, such a button is tied to the **Escape** key in Unity's Input settings (under the "Cancel" submenu).

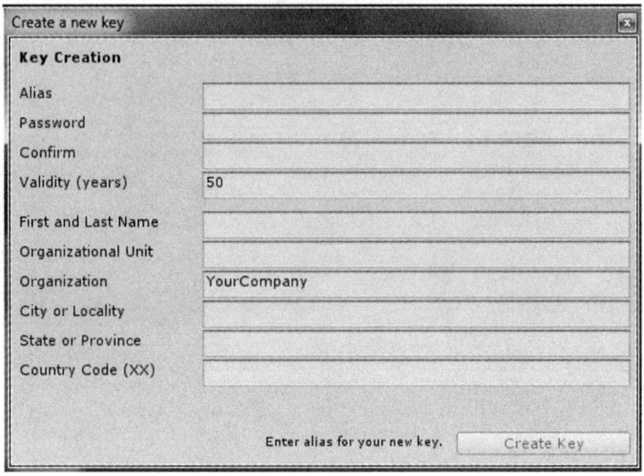

FIGURE 9.6   The data we need to fill for completing the key creation.

All we have to do then is simply add the following code in the **Update()** method of the *GameManager* script to keep checking whether that key gets pressed:

```
void Update() {
            if (Input.GetKey ("escape"))
                 Application.Quit ();
    }
```

If you are working on a Mac and would like to deploy to iPhone Operating System (iOS) instead, the steps to follow within Unity are quite similar: switch to *iOS* as your target platform, and change the *Player Preferences* accordingly (bundle identifier, orientation, minimum iOS version to be supported, etc.). Unity will then build an XCode project for us that we can open and launch to test our game on either the simulator or a real device (assuming we have a valid iOS developer account and all the necessary provisioning profiles installed; see http://docs.unity3d.com/Manual/iphone-GettingStarted.html for more details).

To conclude this chapter, there is one more point that needs to be addressed: regardless of the target platform (Android, iOS, Windows, etc.), we have to be sure that our mobile game is playable on a variety of devices having different screen sizes and form factors. Already, when developing for PC, we can actually test how the game would look by clicking on the

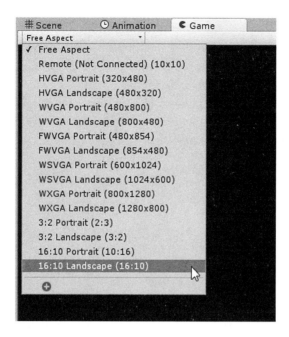

FIGURE 9.7   Be sure to check that the game is playable across different screen ratios!

small drop-down menu in the top right corner of the game view, allowing us to check the viewports for 16:9 and 4:3 screens, for example. This options becomes even more important after changing the target platform to mobile, and Unity will show us several relevant setting for our target of choice (Figure 9.7).

When designing your games and placing all the relevant objects, both in the Game scenes and across the user interface, be sure that nothing of importance could be cut out later on, which can easily happen when carelessly designing the game using a 16:10 viewport but then playing the game in a 4:3 screen!

Alternatively, it is also possible to programmatically rescale things according to the particular device that the game is running on. Unity's Asset Store offers different solutions to this problem, including some ready-made free scripts like the "Fit all screen size" script* that can be used as a reference.

---

* https://www.assetstore.unity3d.com/en/#!/content/22132.

EXERCISE

Currently, pressing the device's Back button will make the game exit, regardless of the scene we are in, since the relevant command has been added to the GameManager object that remains active throughout the game. Modify the relevant Game scripts across the various scenes, so that pressing the Back button on your device quits the game only when in the Main Menu while, in any other scene, it simply takes us back to the Main Menu itself.

III

Developing a 3D Game for PC and VR

CHAPTER 10

Terrain and First Person Character

A FTER HAVING SEEN HOW to develop 2D games and how to deploy them to a mobile device, we can finally move a step further and use all our acquired knowledge to develop a basic 3D game with the ultimate goal of experiencing it in a virtual reality (VR) setting.

Our game will be played from a first-person perspective, with the player lost in a forest and chased by some enemy. It's a very simple setup that will, nonetheless, allow us to introduce a few very important Unity features and related skill sets, starting from terrain generation. Start a new project with the 3D settings selected and, from the GameObject menu, add a *Terrain* (Figure 10.1).

A textureless and completely flat terrain will then be displayed, as in Figure 10.2.

Zoom out so you can have a good overview of the whole terrain, and click on the Terrain cog in the Inspector to showcase all its different settings (Figure 10.3).

Here, we can change different parameters, including the size of the terrain, by default set at 500×500 units. It would make sense to scale our game so that 1 unit equals 1 m, and we can probably leave the default size as it is. Feel free to experiment with a bigger terrain, but be aware that the bigger the terrain and the more assets, like trees and grass, that we add later, the more processing power will be needed in-game, so these shouldn't be overused, especially if we are planning on targeting a mobile platform.

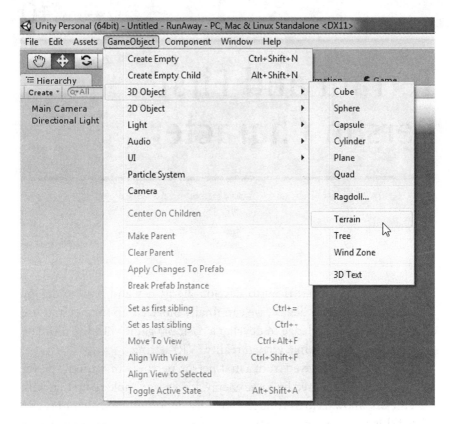

FIGURE 10.1   Adding a terrain to our empty project.

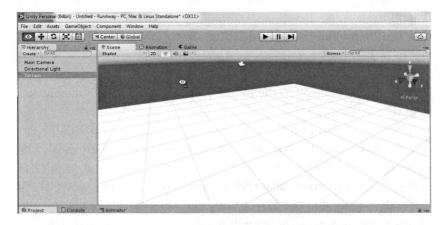

FIGURE 10.2   For moving around the scene view and having a better look at the newly created terrain, we can also use the so-called flythrough mode: right click on the mouse and then press the WASD keys, just like in any PC FPS game, to move around. Press "Shift" together with the movement keys, to "run" faster.

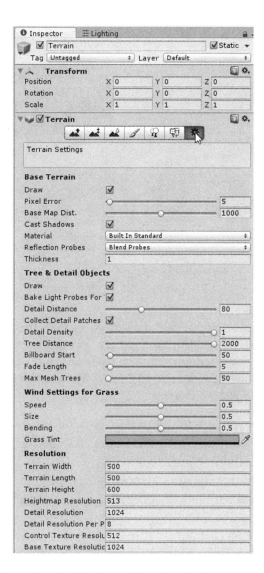

FIGURE 10.3   Accessing the Terrain settings. Resolution, size, and other settings related to trees, and how wind can bend grass, can be changed here.

A white, flat terrain doesn't make much sense, though, so let's start by adding some texture to it. The *Environment* asset pack (included in the Standard Assets) has all we need. To import it, select it as shown in Figure 10.4.*

---

* Importing all the suggested packages will likely include assets you will not need. Nevertheless, unless you know exactly what to use and what the dependencies are, importing everything is a safer way to proceed without risking errors and warning messages later.

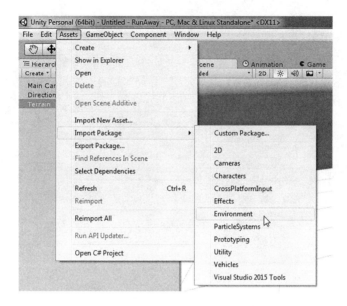

FIGURE 10.4 Importing the Environment assets from the Standard Assets. These are usually downloaded together with Unity. If you don't have them installed already, you can download them for free from the Unity Asset Store. Once imported, a new "Standard Assets" folder will be added to the Project tab together with its related subfolders.

To add a grass texture to the terrain, click on the Brush icon shown among the Inspector components in Figure 10.3. The Terrain component will then change, like in Figure 10.5.

It is important that we familiarize ourselves with the tools at our disposal here. A set of brushes with different shapes can be selected to "paint" the underlying terrain. Each of these not only has its unique drawing pattern but can also be customized further through the **Settings** sliders: in fact, we can change the brush *size*, its *opacity* (how transparent a single pass of the brush will be, a value of "0" meaning invisible), and its *strength*. All these are fundamental to merge different textures into a natural-looking mix, breaking any repetitive pattern that will be created when tiling the same small texture over and over.

To actually add the first texture, click on the **Edit Textures** button. This will open a new window like in Figure 10.6, through which we can select any previously imported texture that was in the Environment assets (Figure 10.7).

Let's pick a texture suitable for uniformly covering the ground (note that the first texture we choose will automatically cover the whole terrain).

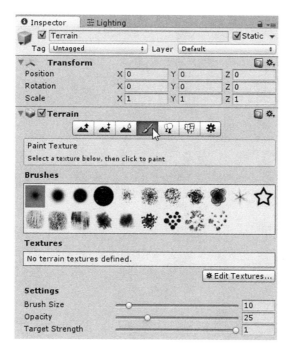

FIGURE 10.5   The Brush icon allows us to add textures and use different brushes to create natural-looking terrains.

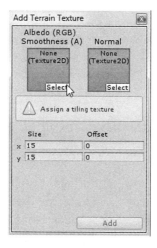

FIGURE 10.6   Adding textures. Each texture may also have a normal map associated to it. Normal maps define how each point in the texture should reflect incoming light and can be a very effective way of simulating rough surfaces, giving an idea of 3D, even though the texture is actually just a plain 2D image.

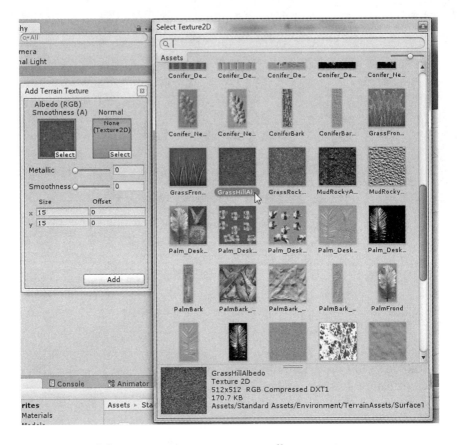

FIGURE 10.7   Selecting a grass texture to cover all our terrain.

Once done, let's also add two more textures, one with some rocks and that can also showcase a normal map, like "MudRocky" (all of these are shown next to each other in Figure 10.7).

We now have enough textures to actually draw an interesting terrain: have fun experimenting for a short while with the different brush types, and see what you can get!

Once you feel familiar using the different brushes, we can move on and check out the tools for raising and lowering the terrain, which are accessible via the three icons at the left of the brush in Figure 10.5.

Selecting the first icon turns all available brushes into tools for shaping hills and mountains of various sizes. How fast the hills grow is determined, in this case, by the opacity parameter: set it to 100, and you will have some scary peak growing up in no time! Much lower opacity values are recommended to carefully build up a more natural-looking scenario.

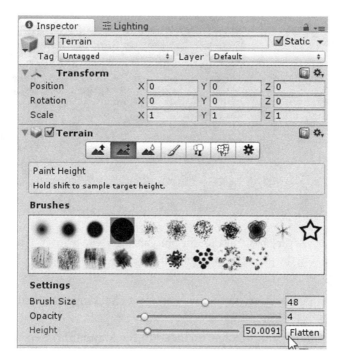

FIGURE 10.8   Thanks to the Paint Height settings, we can draw mountains that will top at a predefined maximum height (think of a chopped-off cone like a volcano). Note, also, that a newly added terrain always starts from a height of 0, and flattening it to a different height via the Flatten button makes for a handy offset that allows us to proceed in both directions: not only drawing mountains upward, but also sculpting downward to create canyons and beds for rivers and lakes.

Pressing Shift together with the left mouse button will instead lower an existing terrain: mountains can be lowered, and canyons or beds for rivers and lakes can be created, as well. By default, though, a terrain starts at a 0 level, and to create a canyon, for example, we have to raise the whole terrain first. This is done easily, by fixing a new offset height via a slider under the second icon ("Paint Height"), as shown in Figure 10.8, followed by pressing the **Flatten** button. The whole terrain will then be set at the height specified, allowing us to actually dig into it if needed.

Since our playing area, as defined by our terrain, will be limited to a surface of 500 m^2, we don't want the player to clearly see the "end of the world," and we should probably block his or her view by raising some mountain chain all around the playing perimeter (Figure 10.9).

Once this is done, and you are happy with how your terrain looks so far, it would be good to add a character we can move around from a

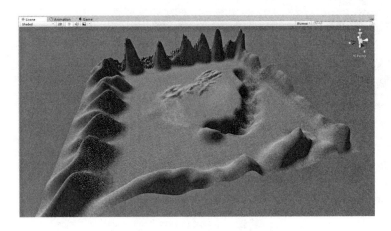

FIGURE 10.9   A very basic terrain for our gaming scene, with hills and mountains preventing the player from falling off the edges of the map.

first-person perspective, so that we can start checking how actually moving around feels.

Unity's *Characters* package, included in the Standard Assets, offers different ready-to-use prefabs, including a handy *first person controller* perfect for a game like ours. Import the package like we did earlier (we will use the "Third Person Character" later, for the zombies, but feel free to discard the "Roller Ball" controllers if you like).

A new set of folders will then appear within the Assets main folder in the Project tab. Look for the *Prefabs* subfolder in the *First Person Character* folder. There will be two prefabs: pick the *FPSController* and bring it into your scene somewhere above the ground (Figure 10.10).

Since the FPSController has its own camera, we should actually delete the one that Unity added by default when we first created our game. Testing the game now allows us to explore our little map in a proper first-person style, using WASD keys for movement, SHIFT for running, and SPACE for jumping, while the mouse controls the direction we are looking to. Exit the game (press ESC to regain control of the mouse pointer after the game started if you are stuck in the Game window) and check the Inspector tab for the FPSController to see how it works (Figure 10.11).

Besides Rigidbody (set to Kinematic) and AudioSource components, we also have a script and a Character Controller component exposing a series of public variables, allowing us to modify how the controller will actually play later in the game. Note, in particular, the variables related to *walk/ run* speed and jumping in the script. The *slope limit* variable is also an

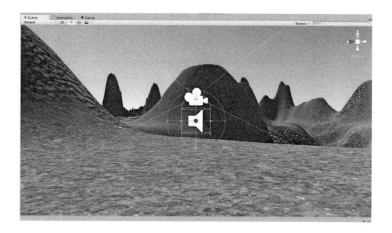

FIGURE 10.10 Bringing the FPSController into a scene. The set of gizmos and wireframes already tells us a few important things about the new object: it has audio and a camera, besides a capsule collider.

important one, as it determines the maximum slope inclination that our character will be able to climb up. The *radius* and *height*, instead, refer to the capsule collider seen in Figure 10.10.

We can now try to make our map a little more attractive by adding trees, grass, and water. All these are made quite straightforward by Unity, so let's see how we can proceed.

In the Terrain Inspector tab, next to the Brush icon, we have the **Place Trees** icon. Once selected, an **Edit Trees** button will appear (Figure 10.12), through which we can access any Tree prefab we have loaded into the project (Figure 10.13).

Once one or more tree types have been loaded into the terrain, these will be displayed in Inspector (exactly like the grass and rocky textures we used earlier), together with a few settings that we can manipulate to customize the environment in the way we see fit. In particular, as shown in Figure 10.14, we can change the radius of the area to plant new trees (*Brush Size*), the density of such trees within the that area (*Tree Density*), and their height (*Tree Height*), which can be randomized and set within a predefined range. Pressing the **Mass Place Trees** button instead will ask us for the number of trees we want to place uniformly across the scene.

Growing grass can be added by selecting the icon to the left of the trees in the Terrain Inspector component, named **Paint Details** (Figure 10.15). Once a suitable texture has been selected, grass strains can be added to the terrain in a way very similar to what we did earlier for the trees, providing

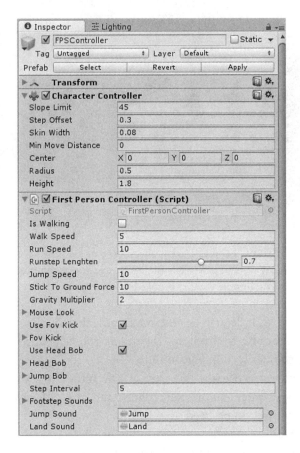

FIGURE 10.11   Some of the components making up the FPSController. Most of the values we need to define how the character will play in the game are accessible via the "Character Controller" and the "First Person Controller" script. Sounds to be played are also defined here.

a much nicer and more natural result (Figure 10.16). Note also that, most likely, if you try to add grass from a distance, you won't see anything being added—but fret not: the grass is actually being created, but the drawn distance limit used by Unity to improve performance won't allow for it to be displayed. This can be changed from the terrain's Settings icon: look for the **Detail Distance** slider in the **Tree & Detail Object** section, and change it accordingly.

In testing the game, we can also appreciate how the grass is gently moved by the wind. Unity does actually allow us to add a wind object to sway nearby trees, as well: simply select the *Wind Zone* object as shown in Figure 10.17, and set its parameters to create the desired effect.

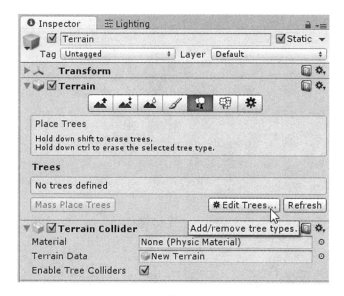

FIGURE 10.12   To add trees to your scene, start by clicking the corresponding icon in the Terrain component.

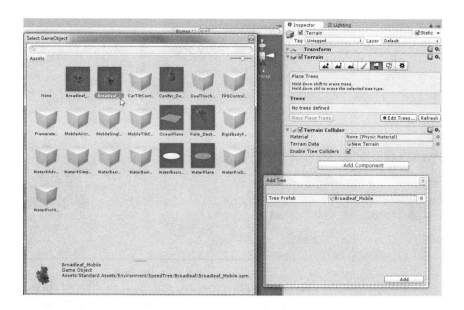

FIGURE 10.13   In the packages we have imported previously, there are a few trees we can freely use in our project.

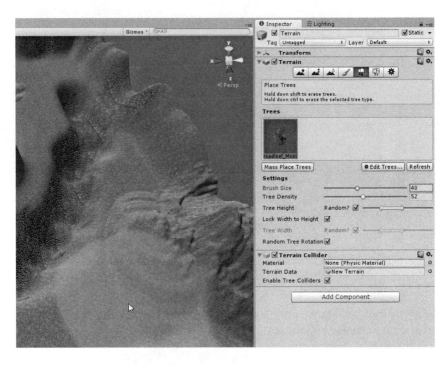

FIGURE 10.14   We can easily change the height, rotation, and density of trees to create varied woods and forests.

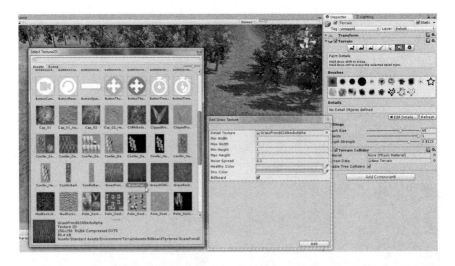

FIGURE 10.15   Adding a texture for grass. Pay attention to the *Billboard* checkbox in the "Add Grass Texture" window: if selected, the texture will always be displayed in front of the player, making it look like a thin 3D object even though, in reality, it's just a simple 2D image.

FIGURE 10.16   Playing the game after having added some grass will make for a much more lifelike experience.

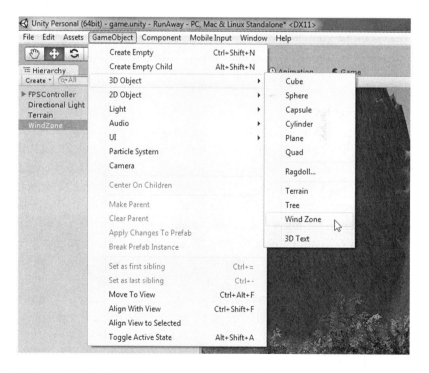

FIGURE 10.17   Adding wind to see trees moving for an even more realistic looking environment is very easily accomplished by adding a Wind Zone object to the Game scene.

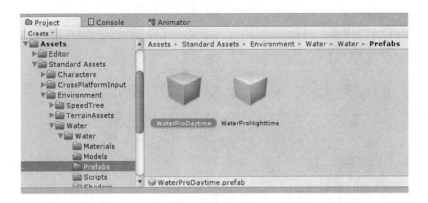

FIGURE 10.18   Adding water to the scene is easily done, thanks to the provided Standard Assets prefabs.

Last, adding water is also very easy in Unity5, thanks to some very good-looking shaders and readily accessible prefabs. In the terrain we created earlier (Figure 10.9), we actually dig a canyon that we can now fill with water. If you don't have anything similar in your own scene, use the terrain sculpting tools to dig a crater or a valley that we can now use to create a lake or a small river. Head down in the Project folders hierarchy and look for the Water prefab folder (Figure 10.18). Here, we can actually find two prefabs, one specific for daytime and a slightly different one suitable for the night.

Once the prefab matching the time of the day in your scene has been added, we will need to position and scale it so that it overlaps and fills the appropriate areas of our map. The Inspector also shows a few parameters, including a **Water Mode** drop-down list allowing us to select a **Simple** mode (no reflections), **Reflective** mode (the outside environment is reflected by the water surface, but we can't see under the water), and **Refractive** mode (showing, also, what lies under the water surface). We now have all the elements to craft some very good-looking open environments in which to set our gaming action,* like in Figure 10.19!

A word of warning, though: don't overuse these features, as handling all these assets at runtime will definitely impact the game's performance considerably, especially if you are going to target a mobile platform!

---

* Don't try to swim, though: the water is just a simple surface and won't sustain the player's weight!

FIGURE 10.19 Trees moved by a gentle breeze near a lake (with "Water Mode" set to "Refractive"). Note that if you find a nice spot while moving across the scene view and would like to actually move the in-game camera to that specific spot, you can easily do so by selecting the Camera object and then the option "Align with View" from the "Game Object" menu.

CHAPTER 11

Enemies and Path Finding

Now that we have a proper terrain and a moving first-person camera, we can think of adding an enemy who will relentlessly chase after us. To escape, in our simple game prototype, the player will need to find a magical exit placed somewhere in the scene before he or she gets caught by the artificial intelligence (AI) pursuer.

For simplicity, let us use the ready-made AI character provided with the Characters package that we imported in the previous chapter (Figure 11.1). While its name is "Ethan," and it is not really some scary-looking monster or zombie, it will be good enough as a placeholder to understand how we can add enemies smart enough to move around a level and look for a pre-defined target.

Bring Ethan into the scene and select him to see all his components in the Inspector (Figure 11.2). Here, we can see that he has, besides a *Rigidbody* and a *Capsule Collider*, an *Animator* component (Figure 11.3), and something we didn't encounter yet: a *Nav Mesh Agent* component.

This is the component ultimately responsible for the path-finding prowess of our AI and hides all the algorithmic complexity of the search, offering us just a few simple parameters we can fine-tune according to our needs.*

---

* A detailed reference for NavMeshAgent can be found in the Unity documentation.

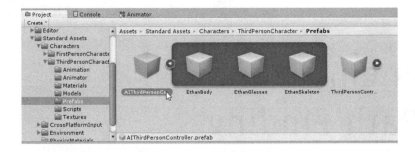

FIGURE 11.1   In the "Third Person Character" folder, we can find a rigged and animated AI character named Ethan that we can use to test our game.

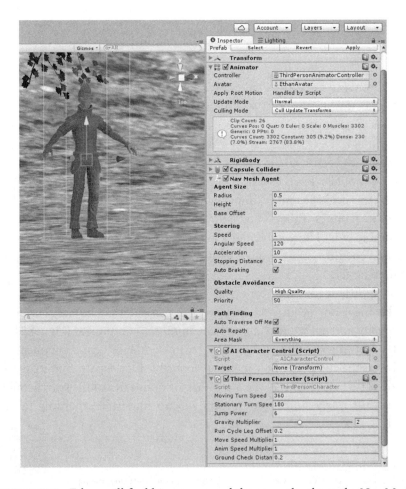

FIGURE 11.2   Ethan will find his way around the scene thanks to the Nav Mesh Agent component. Targeting a specific object and actual movement are handled by supporting scripts like "AI Character Control" and "Third Person Character."

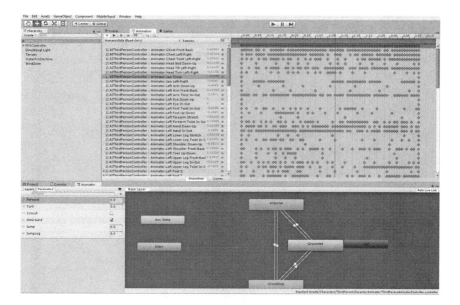

FIGURE 11.3   Ethan's Animator component. Ethan has three main states (Airborne, Crouched, and Grounded), each with different animations that can be blended together as needed. Clicking on each state reveals the corresponding Animation blend tree used to morph between different motions. (Discussing animation and blend trees is beyond the scope of this book, but the interested reader can check http://docs.unity3d.com/Manual/class-BlendTree.html to find out more.)

Of particular importance is the target parameter in the AI Character Control script: drag and drop our FPSController there from the Hierarchy to specify that we want the player to be the character that Ethan has to chase.

We are not done yet, though, and trying to run the game at this stage will only bring up a static Ethan stuck in his idle animation, plus an error message notifying us that there is no *nav mesh* yet. "Nav mesh," short for "navigation mesh," is a procedure that maps the whole terrain mesh according to some predefined criteria to identify where an AI character is allowed, and is not allowed, to walk. To set this up, select the Terrain in Hierarchy and then open the Window/Navigation menu (Figure 11.4). This will open up a *Navigation* tab like in Figure 11.5.

The Navigation tab will include three sections: *Object* (our terrain should already be selected, showing also a drop-down list to specify the navigation area to analyze), *Bake* (where we can define the movement limitations we want to associate our characters), and *Areas* (where we

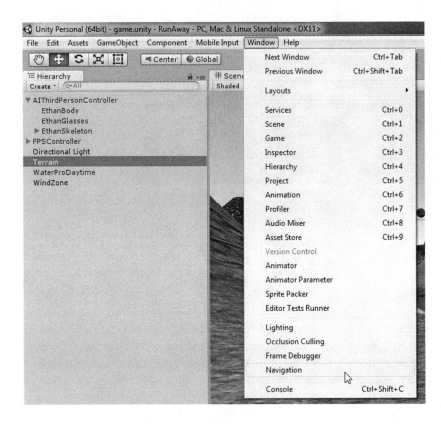

FIGURE 11.4   Adding a nav mesh to an existing terrain.

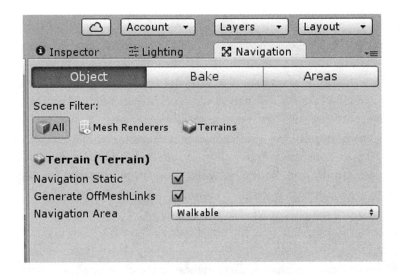

FIGURE 11.5   The Navigation tab.

can specify "costs" for specific parts of the terrain). The latter is related to how the path-finding algorithm actually works: to decide the best path between the current and the goal position, it has to evaluate some sort of "cost" involved across all the different options and then pick the cheapest one. For example, we could have a possible path where we move on plain grass and one where we have to go through ponds and a river instead, so we can force the AI to pick the former by specifying that crossing the river will involve a higher "cost." Anyway, adding and modifying these won't be necessary in this context, and what we need to do instead is to focus our attention on the Bake part (Figure 11.6). This is where we actually specify the limitations that the AI has to take into account during movement, like the effective size of the AI to be used for the nav mesh computation (*agent's radius and height*), the maximum inclination the AI can climb (*max slope*), the small height differences it can step on (*step*

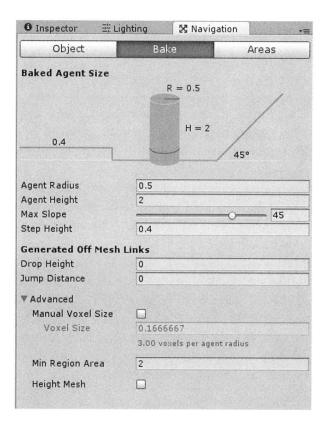

FIGURE 11.6   In the Baking section, we can define relevant criteria for the path-finding search algorithm.

FIGURE 11.7 Terrain with nav mesh. Ethan is standing next to a tree, and we can see how the latter is not included in the nav mesh (i.e., lighter area in the picture) and is considered as an obstacle, meaning that Ethan won't be able to go through it but will have to circumnavigate it if necessary.

height), and how finely the terrain should be segmented during the analysis (the parameters in the "Advanced" submenu). Note also the section named **Off Mesh Links**. These will allow automatic generation of specific points where the AI can move across even if the nav mesh is not continuous, effectively linking different areas of the nav mesh. Think of jumping through a crevasse, for example.

In our prototype, we can start with the default parameters and see if they work well for the terrain we created so far. Press the **Bake** button at the right bottom corner of the Bake window and, after a short while, you should see the nav mesh appearing as a highlighted area across the terrain (Figure 11.7).*

Playtesting the game will show Ethan moving around and running toward us. This is a good time to improve the terrain further and possibly add some obstacles as well. Let's try to add some boulders and see what happens. Head to http://opengameart.org/content/mossy-stone-rock and download the public domain rock asset. Unzip it and import all files, including OBJ and Texture folder (you can just drag and drop them into the project).†

---

* The Navigation tab must be selected for the nav mesh to appear across the terrain.
† Unity can easily read different 3D file formats. See https://docs.unity3d.com/Manual/3D-formats.html for details.

Bring the Stone model into the scene and place it somewhere in between Ethan and the first-person character.

Right now, the model is untextured, so let's access its material, change its shader to "Bumped Specular," for example, and select a couple of the provided textures, including the rock's normal map (Figure 11.8). Once done, add a box collider to the stone as shown in Figure 11.9.

If the stone is relatively small, Ethan will be able to avoid its collider without issues, but what happens if we make it bigger? Let's make the *x*

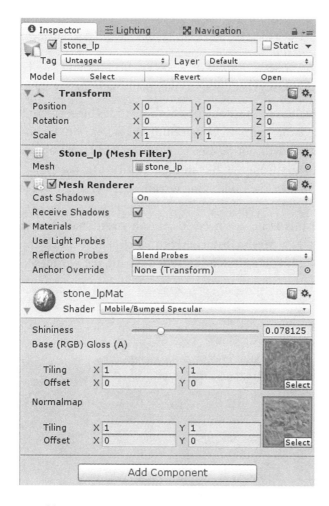

FIGURE 11.8 Adding textures to the Stone material. Since we will ultimately test the prototype on a mobile device, selecting a mobile shader may be a good idea. (Mobile shaders are simplified and optimized versions of commonly used shaders.)

FIGURE 11.9 Don't forget to add a box collider to the stone! Remember, the collider's scale is relative to the object's scale, so changing the latter will also enlarge the former. The stone is strategically placed in between Ethan and the first-person controller to easily check its effect on Ethan's path-finding abilities.

and *y* scale values of the Stone object three times bigger than the original and run the game again. If we place our character right behind the stone, this time Ethan will not be able to circumnavigate the obstacle and will simply try to go through it, like in Figure 11.10. The reason is that the nav mesh still includes the underlying terrain surface, so the not-so-smart AI still sees it as a viable path.

To avoid this issue, we need to add an additional component to the Stone object: **Nav Mesh Obstacle** (Figures 11.11 and 11.12). This will allow the corresponding object to be excluded during the nav mesh search and,

FIGURE 11.10 Sorry, Ethan: No matter how hard you try, you really can't go that way!

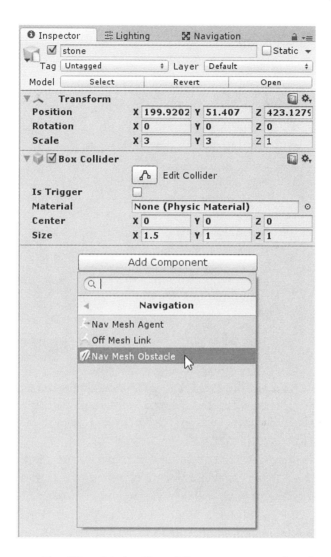

FIGURE 11.11 The "Nav Mesh Obstacle" component is found under the "Navigation" group. We may also want to click on the Static checkbox as the stone won't move or change in any way during the game. This allows Unity to perform some further optimization tasks regarding navigation, lighting, and more.

if the object is static and not moving, the underlying terrain will also be removed from the walkable nav mesh. This is achieved by selecting the Carve checkbox in Figure 11.12, and it is exactly what we need here.

Test the game again now, and Ethan should be able to run around the big stone and reach us.

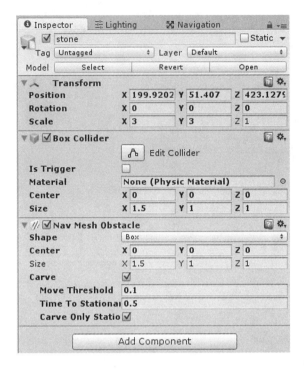

FIGURE 11.12 Make sure that the size and shape of the nav mesh obstacle match the collider! Checking "Carve" is necessary to exclude the terrain under a static object or under an object that has not moved for a certain time ("Time to Stationary").

We can now proceed to add some sort of gate or location that we, as the player, need to reach—before being captured by Ethan—to win the game. Open Game Art can still be a valuable place to search for possible 3D models, and I will pick a Stonehenge-like structure kindly licensed under the public domain by its author.* Download the file, unzip it, and bring the 3D model plus its texture into the project.† Bring the model in the scene somewhere close to the player (for easy testing), scale and rotate it as needed, and change its shader to a simple *Mobile/Diffuse* so that we can apply the texture. Last, let's also add a box collider to the structure and check it as a *trigger* (Figure 11.13).

Having the collider in place allows us to check for the winning condition by adding a very simple script, still to the Stonehenge model, where we check whether the incoming object triggering the collision is tagged

---

* http://opengameart.org/content/4-piece-stonehenge-opendungeons.
† Note that this model was done in Blender, and you may need to rename its extension as ".blend" instead of ".blend1" to properly import it in Unity.

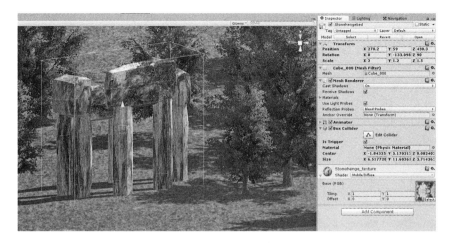

FIGURE 11.13 The imported Stonehenge structure with its various components displayed in the Inspector tab. This will be the stone gates we need to reach to win the game.

as the player. If so, we can proceed accordingly. Tag the FPSController as "Player" in the Inspector, and write the following simple code to the script associated with the Stonehenge model:

```
using UnityEngine;
using System.Collections;

public class StonehengeScript : MonoBehaviour {

void OnTriggerEnter(Collider other) {

  // check for the player:
  if (other.gameObject.tag == "Player") {
    print("Player won!");
    }
  }
}
```

As we see, the script will only output a simple message in the Console window notifying us that the player did, indeed, reach the gate. We can also add a corresponding one for Ethan when he manages to catch us:

```
using UnityEngine;
using System.Collections;
```

```
public class PlayerFoundScript : MonoBehaviour {

  void OnCollisionEnter(Collision other) {

    if (other.gameObject.tag == "Player")
    {
      print("I got you! Game Over!");
    }
  }
}
```

Test the game to check that everything done so far works as expected and then, as an exercise, add and link a couple of new scenes to properly handle the winning event and congratulate the player, as well as the losing scenario where Ethan reaches the player, showing a Game Over message and a button to restart the game.

The next step we can do to improve our prototype is to define a few spawn points where the Stonehenge structure should appear at the beginning of the game. Leaving it in a fixed position, in fact, won't provide any sort of replay value. Luckily, this is something we can fix easily: create a few *empty objects*,* three for example, and place them strategically around your map in the exact location where you would like the structure to appear. Once done, open the Stonehenge script and add the following code:

```
public Transform[] spawn;
void Start() {
  int i = Random.Range(0, spawn.Length);
  this.transform.position = spawn[i].position;
}
```

Here, we are simply declaring a public array named "Spawn" to store any number of *Transform* objects and then, in the *Start()* method, we pick a random element in the array and position the object the script is associated with (i.e., the Stonehenge structure in this case) in the coordinates identified by the element in the array we just picked.

Note something important about the *Random.Range(min, max)* method: there are two versions, one for integers and one for floats. In the latter, both min and max values are included, while in the former only the

---

* "Empty objects" are objects that only have a Transform component, and they can be very useful in marking specific positions, as in this case.

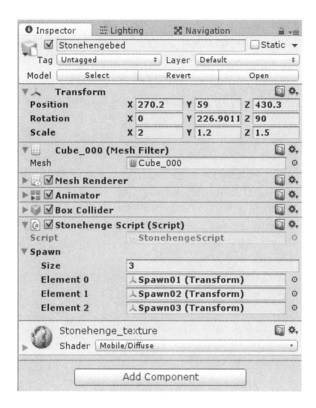

FIGURE 11.14   Spawn points added!

minimum value is included, and the max is excluded (to facilitate its use when working with arrays).

Going back to the *Inspector*, we now have the Spawn array accessible: set its size to 3, and drag and drop all the empty objects we created earlier into the array slots as shown in Figure 11.14.

Play the game and verify that, indeed, the structure initial position is randomized.

We are now ready to add the word "Shooter" to "First Person." Create a new 3D spherical object in the scene (for simplicity, here we are going to shoot basic spherical bullets), name it "Bullet," scale it to have *x*, *y*, and *z* dimensions equal to 0.1, and then add a *Rigidbody* component to it. Since the bullet will travel quite fast, let's change the *collision detection* parameter in the Rigidbody to "Continuous Dynamic."

We can assign the speed of the bullet in a new script that we should create right away. Name it "Bang" (or whatever you like), add it to the Bullet object, and open it for editing, writing the following code:

```
using UnityEngine;
using System.Collections;

public class Bang : MonoBehaviour {
  private Rigidbody rb;
  float thrust = 50f;

  void Start () {
        // get a reference to the rigidbody
        rb = GetComponent< Rigidbody > ();
        // shoot the object, i.e. bullet, with an
impulsive force
        rb.AddForce(transform.forward * thrust,
ForceMode.Impulse);
  }
  void OnCollisionEnter( Collision other) {
        // if we hit Ethan, he will be moved back a
few meters.
        if (other.gameObject.tag == "Ethan" ){
        other.gameObject.transform.position +=
transform.forward*3f ;
        }
  // destroy bullet regardless of object hit
  Destroy ( this.gameObject);
  }
}
```

Here, we define the force that will accelerate our bullet forward (the *thrust* float variable), which is added to the Rigidbody component via the *AddForce()* method.* When a collision event is recorded, we check if we hit Ethan (let's assign a tag to him for simplicity), and then we decide what to do with him: we could just kill/destroy him with some cool explosion effect, make him respawn in a randomly selected position following the same approach we used with the Stonehenge gate, or just push him back a little bit to give us a chance to run away. The script does the latter in a very straightforward way by simply changing his position, but you should try to make things look more spectacular or realistic as an exercise. Last,

---

* "Transform.forward" is the unit vector pointing forward relative to the current object position. Note also how we are using AddForce this time, with the additional ForceMode.Impulse parameter to simulate a proper shot-like event.

the bullet needs to be destroyed, otherwise we will soon have hundreds of bullets running toward infinity and beyond!

Once done, turn this into a prefab and remove it from the scene.

Where should we shoot the bullet from, though? We need a spawn point for this as well, which we can name **Gun** and place as a child object of the camera (which is in "First Person Character") right in front of us, as shown in Figure 11.15.

For actually shooting the bullets, all we need is another simple script attached to the gun that will instantiate a Bullet object (referenced via a public variable from the Inspector) whenever the **Fire1** button is pressed. This, by default, is associated with the left control key and left mouse button, as we can see from the "Edit/Project Settings/Input" menu. Note also how the bullet is spawned not only in the exact position of the Gun object instantiating it but also with the same rotation angles, so that the "forward" axes of the gun and of the bullet are aligned.

```
using UnityEngine;
using System.Collections;

public class ShootingScript : MonoBehaviour {

    public GameObject bullet;
```

FIGURE 11.15   Placing the gun (an empty object here) right in front of the camera. Bullets will be shot from here.

```
void Update () {
  if (Input.GetButtonDown("Fire1")) {
  // create a new bullet in the scene at this very
location
  Instantiate(bullet, this.transform.
position, this.transform.rotation);
  }
 }
}
```

With our first-person prototype now working, we can end this chapter by discussing a few eye candies to polish the overall game. For example, given the eerie nature of this game, where we are chased by one or more enemies (try adding more "Ethans" if you like, making the escape more difficult), such an idyllic atmosphere may be a little out of place. Maybe adding some fog would help us to create tension and suspense. From the *Window* menu, select *Lighting* (Figure 11.16). Here we have, among several different components, a

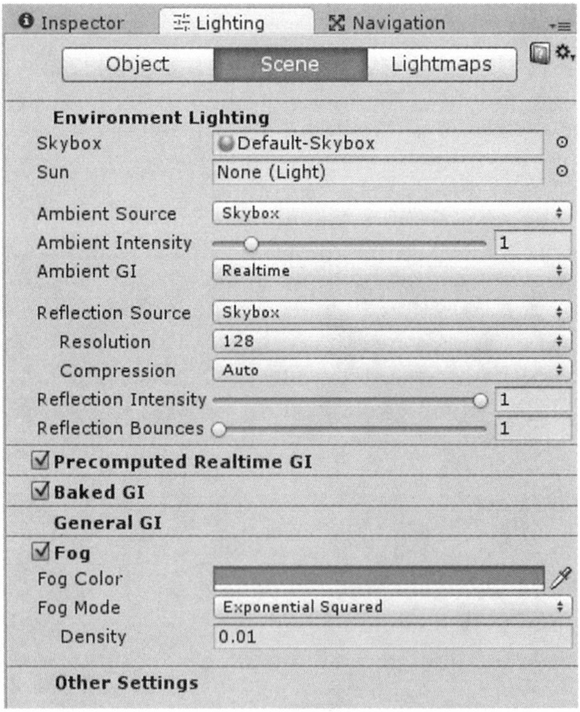

FIGURE 11.16 The Lighting tab. Note that if no "Sun" is explicitly selected, the brightest directional light source in the scene will automatically be selected for us.

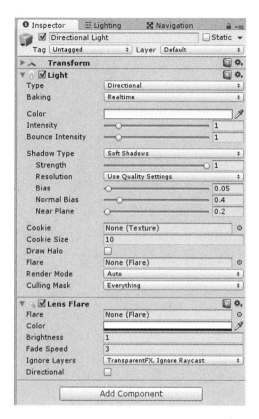

FIGURE 11.17   Properties of the directional light in the scene after having added a Lens Flare component.

Fog option that we can activate and then customize as we please by selecting its color, how it should decay with distance, and its density. Try different settings and see which one looks best in your environment.

Lens flares are also a nice effect that are common in modern games, so let's add one here as well. Select the directional light acting as the sun in our scene and add a new **Lens Flare** component to it (Figure 11.17). In the "Flare" field, though, we won't have anything to select yet, and we need to import another package, named **Effects**, from the Standard Assets like we did previously from the "Assets/Import Package" menu. Once done, we will have a few different flares at our disposal. Pick one and check the "Directional" checkbox.

In the scene view, the flare effect should now appear whenever we look at the sun. If it doesn't, be sure that "Flares" is marked as visible in the scene's picture icon drop-down menu (Figure 11.18).

FIGURE 11.18   While in the scene view, we can easily turn skyboxes, fog, and flares on/off.

Nonetheless, to actually see the effect in the game, we need to do one more step: a *Flare Layer* component, in fact, has also to be added to the game camera (which is in our first-person character) for the effect to be actually visible in-game.

Lighting effects can do a lot in terms of building the right atmosphere. Likewise, sound is also extremely powerful: since we added the wind effect earlier, we should now end this chapter by adding a wind sound as well. Search the web for a suitable loopable wind sound clip you can freely use (opengameart.org and freesfx.co.uk are good starting points). Once you have imported the sound, add a new empty object to *FPSController*, and then add an *AudioSource* component to it.* This audio source can then be used to play the wind SFX we downloaded (Figure 11.19).

---

* Don't use the sound source already included in the FPSController itself, since this will be used by the Controller scripts for the character footsteps.

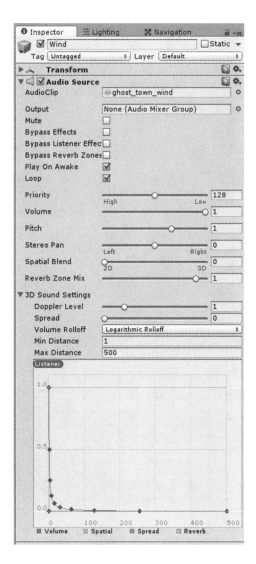

FIGURE 11.19   The wind SFX should start playing right away (check "Play on Awake") and loop. Since we have only one big open scene, it makes sense to attach it to the player so that the blowing wind is perfectly audible everywhere. In this case, though, the 3D sound settings won't do anything. If, instead, we had a sound attached to a moving object relative to the listener, we could actually simulate some realistic sound properties, like volume rolloff and Doppler effects, by changing the parameters provided herein.

CHAPTER 12

Introduction to VR and Google Cardboard

V IRTUAL REALITY (VR), OR the simulation of an actual physical presence in a virtual world, has been in the works for a long time. Stanley Weinbaum's 1935 science-fiction novel *Pygmalion's Spectacles* described a goggle-based device able to immerse its wearer in an alternative dimension, and the term was first adopted as early as 1938 in Antonin Artaud's book *Le Theatre et son double* to describe the illusionary nature of characters in a theatrical setting.

As soon as technology was advanced enough to produce moving stereoscopic images able to trick our brains into seeing 3D objects, the race to immerse ourselves in artificially created worlds began. The 1990s were particularly significant for building hype around VR: several blockbuster movies* were produced, and game-related devices like the ill-fated Nintendo Virtual Boy (Figure 12.1) were commercialized.

It was only recently, though, and mostly thanks to the push contributed by the crowdfunded Oculus Rift headset project, that VR moved from an academic research interest and sci-fi curiosity to an actual product affordable enough to be successfully commercialized on a mass production scale.

Among all the different headsets that followed the Oculus Rift, Google Cardboard† is perhaps the most surprising for its minimalist approach

---

* For example, see *The Lawnmower Man* (1992), *Johnny Mnemonic* (1995), and *Nirvana* (1997).

† For more information on Google Cardboard, including models to buy online, check https://developers.google.com/cardboard/.

FIGURE 12.1   Nintendo was the first gaming giant to push a VR-based system in 1995. Unfortunately, times and technology were not yet mature.

and cheap price, allowing anyone with a mid-range smartphone to easily experience VR for the first time.

A Cardboard (Figure 12.2) is, in fact, nothing more than an empty shell wrapping a smartphone that is playing a suitably rendered VR application, where head movements are tracked via a gyrometer. By default, the only input device is a simple button, which, in the early Cardboard models, was simulated by sliding a neodymium disk over a ceramic magnet placed on the side of the Cardboard itself. When moved, the resulting magnetic field change would be measured by the magnetometer used by the phone's own compass functionality and would trigger an event that programmers could identify and use.

Google is constantly working on expanding and improving the Cardboard experience, including additional peripherals like the "Daydream Controller," a motion-sensing device able to track movement in 3D space,

FIGURE 12.2   Second-generation Google Cardboard. Notice the button on the right. In the early models, this wasn't present, and instead there was a sliding magnet on the left side of the device.

besides adding traditional button inputs.* Anyway, this controller will likely remain an optional component, as there are already millions of Cardboards around the world. In this context, we will focus on the core experience involving the basic Cardboard setup only. Be aware, too, that there are Cardboards based on several different designs, including some that don't even have a button. This may sound a bit surprising at first, but this limitation can be easily overcome, and events can still be triggered, for example, by staring at a specific object for a certain amount of time.

Moving to Unity5, our game engine of choice has very handy built-in functionalities for VR and can support a variety of devices. To enable VR support, though, first and foremost we must select the **Virtual Reality Supported** checkbox in *Player Preferences* (Figure 12.3). Once done, Unity will be able to render the main camera in stereoscopic mode on exporting to the targeted device, while also computing all the relevant mathematical transformations needed to display the scenes according to the inputs from the head-tracking sensors.

---

* The latest software development kit (SDK) also includes a demo scene explaining how to use such a controller. Related documentation can be found here: https://developers.google.com/vr/unity/get-started-controller.As the SDk continues to evolve, I would recommend learning the fundamentals by following this chapter along with the Headset demo scene provided in the "Cardboard_DemoForUnity. unitypackage" available for download from http://ProgramAndPlay.com. Only after the basics are well understood, update the SDK to check any additional features/changes in the latest version.

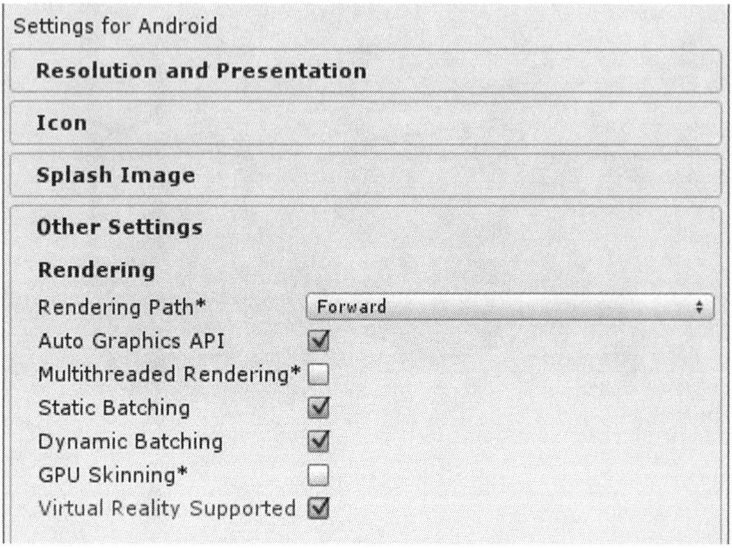

FIGURE 12.3   To enable VR in Unity, we need to navigate to the "Project Settings/Player" under the "Edit Menu" and then, in the "Other Settings" for our platform of choice, check the "Virtual Reality Supported" flag to enable VR mode in the Inspector. Since Unity 5.4.0, it is also possible to explicitly include one or more particular devices here (like Oculus) or to specify more generic setups (like a stereo display).

To develop VR games playable in any Google Cardboard compatible device, we need first to download the Unity-Cardboard SDK from http://bit.ly/1Sezv81, together with a simple demo app that can show us how things work out.*

Having downloaded both the SDK and Demo Unity packages (note that the Cardboard SDK contains plug-ins for both Android and iOS), import them in a new, clean project and proceed to open the demo scene found in the Cardboard folder (Figure 12.4).

If we run the demo right away, we will see a stereoscopic image like in Figure 12.5. Here, to simulate head movements, we need to press ALT (to look around) or CTRL (to tilt) while moving the mouse. Mouse left click will work as the button/magnet slider.

Feel free also to switch the building platform to Android and test the demo directly on your smartphone.†

---

* The latest build can be found here: https://github.com/googlevr/gvr-unity-sdk.
† Refer back to Chapter 9 on how to set up Android SDK on your computer. If you prefer to deploy to iOS instead of Android, check https://developers.google.com/cardboard/unity/get-started-ios for detailed instructions.

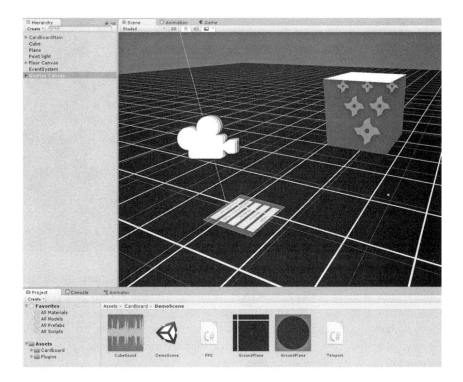

FIGURE 12.4   The demo VR scene included in the "DemoForUnity" package: a cube with particles and a "Floor Canvas" with a few menu items.

Now that we have seen the demo in practice, let's try to understand how it is structured and how it works.

In the Hierarchy, we can see different objects (Figure 12.6), including **Cardboard Main**. (Note that, with the release of the Daydream controller, all generic "Cardboard" components have been renamed as GoogleVR or Gvr so, according to the specific SDK version you are using, "Cardboard Main" may be now called "GvrMain.") This is at the heart of the VR experience and is an instance of the corresponding prefab, which is made of two more objects: **Head**, which includes the main camera, now split into two stereoscopic cameras, one for each eye, plus the cardboard reticle; and a **Stereo Render**, an instance of the Cardboard/Gvr Manager prefab to properly handle the rendering process. If we zoom into the Cardboard main object, we will actually see three camera gizmos: one for the "main" camera and one each for the left and right eye.

Notice also how **Cardboard Main/Gvr** has attached a script (named either Cardboard or Gvr Viewer), which automatically enables VR mode in

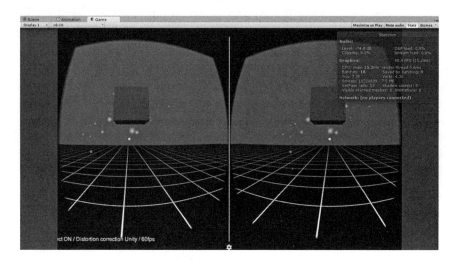

FIGURE 12.5 Testing the Cardboard VR demo in Unity. To interact with the cube, we first need to center it in our view, aiming at it with a small gaze pointer (in the picture, the gaze pointer is the small white dot under the cube). This will make it change color from red to green and then, if we click on it, the cube will respawn elsewhere. If we look down, we will also see a simple menu system that we can interact with in the very same way.

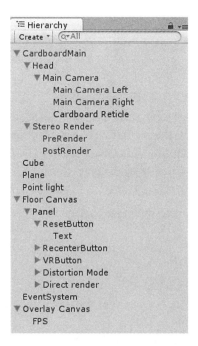

FIGURE 12.6 The Hierarchy in the Cardboard demo project.

Unity and takes care of setting many important parameters for us, besides allowing us to simulate different Cardboard models and phone screens while still testing in Unity (Figure 12.7). Head tracking, meanwhile, is handled in the **Cardboard/Gvr Head** script component of the child **Head** object.

Another very important point to note is the presence in the **Event System** object of an additional **Gaze Input Module** script, besides Unity's own **Touch Input Module**. Thanks to that, not only will touch/button events be recognized, but we will also have the ability to select Canvas elements simply by looking at them.

When starting a new VR game, the first thing we should do is substitute the default main camera with an instance of the **Cardboard (or Gvr) Main** prefab since, as we have just seen, it contains all we need to have a stereo rig plus an instance of the Cardboard script for properly handling the VR mode. This is exactly what we will be doing in the next chapter to adapt our First Person Shooter (FPS) prototype.

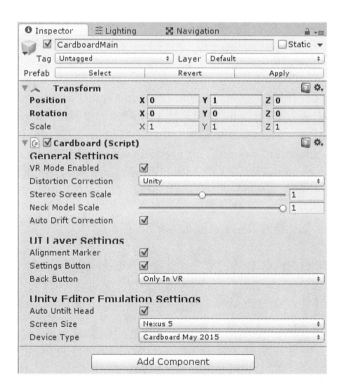

FIGURE 12.7   The Cardboard script (renamed as Gvr Viewer in the latest SDK) sets some important default values for us.

On the other hand, if we are updating a complex non-VR game to a VR setup where a straightforward camera change could break existing scripts already in place, we may want to try adding the **Cardboard/Gvr Adapter** prefab as a child of the main camera, so that the "Cardboard Head" would be under the main camera and not the other way round. In this way, only the stereo cameras, and not the whole camera system, would be affected by the head-motion tracking, which will be enabled once we call the **Update Stereo Cameras** command. The latter is accessible via either the **Stereo Controller** script component of the Main Camera object (Figure 12.8) or via the Context menu (Component/Cardboard/Update Stereo Cameras) that appeared after importing the Cardboard plug-in.* Its role is to take care of resynchronizing the stereo cameras with the main camera whenever needed.

Alternatively, another easy way to start adding VR support to a new scene is simply to attach the **Stereo Controller** script to the default main camera so that it will generate a stereo rig for us when we click the **Update Stereo Cameras** button in the Inspector.

You may want to try this right now: add a new scene to the project, attach the script to the default main camera, and click the button. Playing the scene should now show a working stereoscopic display!

Once a **Cardboard/Gvr Reticle** object from the corresponding prefab (located in the Prefabs/UI subfolder) is added as an additional child to the **GvrMain/Head/MainCamera** object, we can start adding any user interface (UI) elements we want to interact with. Like in the original demo, the corresponding **Event System** also needs a **Gaze Input Module** script for the interaction to work properly,† but all this is not enough and, to set up a VR-ready graphical user interface (GUI), we do need to fully understand how the *Canvas Render Mode works.*

A canvas has three Render mode options:

- *Screen Space–Overlay*: With this option selected, the canvas is scaled to fit the screen and rendered directly as a static overlay image on top of the camera view. Anything displayed on the canvas has a

---

* Note that, in the latest SDK, the context menu has been renamed as "Component/GoogleVR/ Update Stereo Cameras." Check https://developers.google.com/vr/unity/ for more information on the plug-in itself.
† If needed, move the GazeInputModule script up in the EventSystem object's Inspector window by clicking on the setting gear and choosing "move up:" it should be above other modules such as "Touch Input Module" and "Standalone Input Module" components listed, as listing order determines the component priority!

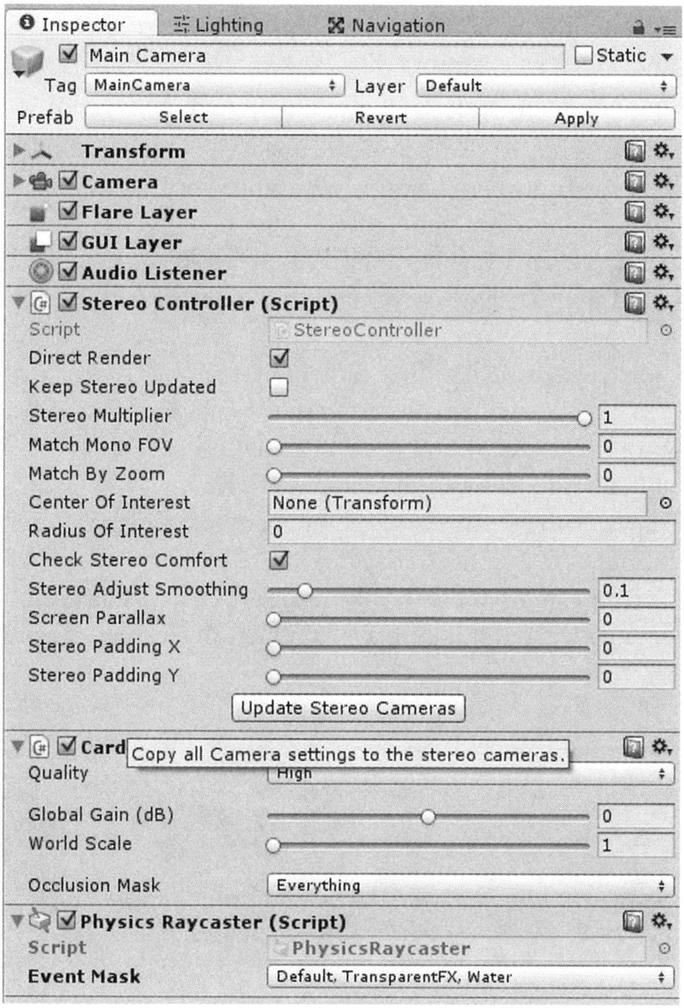

FIGURE 12.8   Components of the Main Camera object. Note the Update Stereo Cameras button in the Stereo Controller script as well as the presence of a Physics Raycaster, which allows the reticle to interact with 3D objects, like the cube in the demo scene, as long as these have colliders and event trigger interfaces to signal specific events.

fixed position and doesn't follow the camera as it moves around. This is what we want when we need to display a typical head-up display (HUD) including things like score, time, number of lives, and so on.

- *Screen Space–Camera*: A variation of the previous mode where the canvas is drawn on a plane some distance in front of a given camera, meaning there can be objects in front of it, and it won't necessarily always be on top like in the previous mode.

- *World Space*: The UI is rendered as if it were a plane within the scene. In other words, it will be rendered as a part of the scene, and its view will be dependent on the camera's relative position and distance.

In our Cardboard VR application, with a stereo camera display and a single button able to trigger only events that are exactly in front of us, this has some important consequences.

First, our rig provides a dual camera system, but we have only one overlay canvas. This will be split between the left- and right-eye cameras, meaning we need to copy and paste any GUI element across the overlay accordingly, so as to have one in each camera view.

Zooming out the main scene of the Cardboard demo will show an "FPS" text right outside the overlay (Figure 12.9).

As an exercise, move the text fully inside the canvas, if needed, and run the scene to verify that it is displayed only on the left-eye camera. Then,

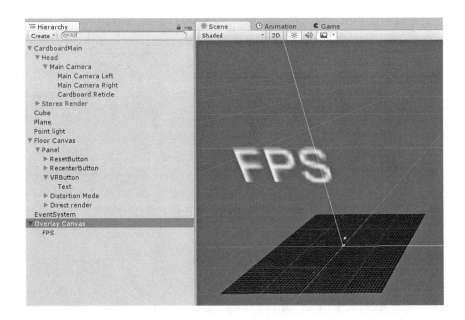

FIGURE 12.9 FPS text in the canvas overlay of the demo project. Every GUI element in the overlay has to be replicated if we want them to be displayed properly for both eyes.

duplicate it and place the clone in the corresponding location of the other screen half, so that it is also properly displayed by the right-eye camera.

The consequence of having only one trigger in a fixed central position for accessing GUI elements is that now we have to design our GUI so that clickable elements like buttons are placed in a different canvas set to **World Space** instead.

Check carefully how this is accomplished in the demo (Figure 12.10) with a "Floor Canvas" containing a panel with various buttons. These are not visible when the demo starts, but we have to look for them by rotating the camera accordingly.

The actual interaction with 3D objects in the scene happens thanks to the inclusion of an additional script, **Physics Raycaster**, which has to be added to the main, stereo camera that the player will be controlling (see Figure 12.8). This will cast "rays" from the pointer toward the direction we are facing but, by itself, it is not enough: we also have to set the receiving objects in a way that they can provide feedback when their colliders have been hit by the ray. This can be achieved by adding a collider and an *Event Trigger* component to the specific object, that is, the Cube in the demo (Figure 12.11).

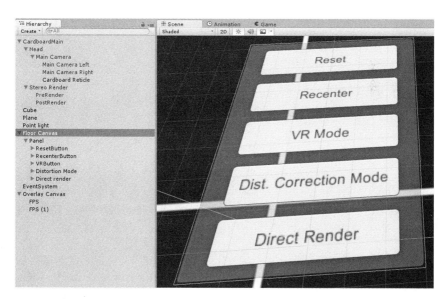

FIGURE 12.10   We need to face clickable items directly to operate them via the trigger in Google Cardboard, meaning that we need to place such GUI elements like buttons in a "World Space"-type canvas instead of in a typical overlay as we have done so far in our other games.

FIGURE 12.11 The Inspector tab for the Cube object in the demo, where we can see its Event Trigger part, defining Enter, Exit, and Click pointer events. These are then handled in the Teleport script.

The events defined for the cube allow it to change color from red to green whenever we are pointing at it and move it to a random nearby location if we click it. All these are triggered by calling the methods defined in the *Teleport* script, which is also a component of the Cube object itself.*

---

* If things don't work as expected, check that there are no layers blocking the raycasts by opening the "Blocking Mask" drop-down menu in any raycaster (e.g., the canvas's graphics raycaster).

CHAPTER 13

Porting to VR

Having clarified how Google Cardboard works and how to set up a virtual reality (VR) project in Unity, we are finally ready to turn our attention back to the 3D First Person Shooter (FPS) prototype that we worked on in Part 3 and adapt it into a VR mobile game project.

First of all, though, I would recommend backing up the existing 3D PC-based project and working on a different copy, where we may want to work on a smaller terrain map and simplify things a little bit for performance reasons. For example, we should probably remove the wind and clean the terrain from most of the grass and some trees (especially in the case when we added a jungle-like vegetation while prototyping in Chapter 11), since these can cause serious frame rate drops and even crashes on not-so-powerful mobile platforms.

To turn our game into a VR project, we will proceed as follows: first, we will modify the camera to enable stereoscopic rendering, and then we will have to rework the first-person controller as the player movement will need to be completely rethought according to the Cardboard platform. Last but not least, we will also add a new Splash screen scene enabling us to switch VR mode on or off.

As we discussed in the previous chapter, once we have imported the Cardboard software development kit (SDK) package in our project, we should substitute the main camera with the **Cardboard/Gvr Main** prefab. To do so, feel free to delete all the *FPSController* children that we had previously (including the camera and the gun*), and then add the VR prefab

---

* Although it is an extremely simple object, you may want to turn the gun into a prefab before deleting it so that you can re-add it easily later.

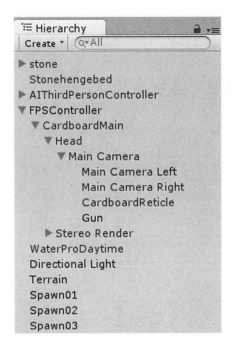

FIGURE 13.1   The Hierarchy structure after removing the original "First Person Character" in FPSController (which had the main camera) and adding the "Cardboard Main" prefab instead (or the GvrMain prefab, according to your specific SDK version). A Reticle object and a simple gun, like the one we had previously, were also added as children to the Main Camera object.

as a new child. Make also a new gun as a child of the new main camera in **Head/MainCamera** and add a **Cardboard/Gvr Reticle** object as well. The scene hierarchy should now look like in Figure 13.1.

Try to play the game now. The stereoscopic display will work great!

We need to think how to move now. Since we will be playing on mobile (remember to change the target platform in the Build settings*) with the Cardboard and no keyboard, the **First Person Controller** script won't be of much help, and we need to think of an alternative solution. We should still keep the script active, though, as it will work together with the Character Controller to take care of the various collisions with the terrain and trees.

How to move, then? The easiest possible approach is to have the player move automatically in the direction that he or she is facing. To achieve

---

* If you have all the standard assets imported in the project this will take a long time, so be ready to be patient. Once again, it is highly recommended to simplify the scene as much as possible to start testing on mobile devices not only to reduce build times but also to avoid crashes and performance issues.

this, we should make a new script—let's name it **VRmovement**—that takes the current direction the main camera is facing in, projects that vector on the ground (i.e., the *x,z* plane), and moves the character accordingly along the *z* direction (i.e., forward):

```
using UnityEngine;
using System.Collections;

public class VRmovement : MonoBehaviour {

  public float thrust = 1f;
  public Camera cam;

  void Update()
  {
    // move in the direction the camera is facing
    Vector3 moveTowards = cam.transform.forward;
    // project vector on xz plane
    moveTowards = Vector3.
ProjectOnPlane (moveTowards, Vector3.up);

    moveTowards.x = moveTowards.x * thrust *
Time.deltaTime;
    moveTowards.z = moveTowards.z * thrust * Time.
deltaTime;
    // we don"t need to add the y component unless we
want to hike over the hills!

    transform.position += moveTowards;
  }
}
```

This script should then be added as a new component to the existing FPSController object, while the *Camera cam* object exposed here should be associated with the *Main Camera* down the hierarchy in the FPSController itself. The *thrust* variable indicates the speed that we want the first-person character to move at.

As we can see, we take the camera forward from its transform and then project it onto the ground *x,z* plane, which is easily identified by the predefined *up* vector (i.e., (0,1,0)).

The components of the movement vectors along the *x* and *z* axes (i.e., to move horizontally and forward/backward in the game space) are then multiplied by thrust and the usual *Time.deltaTime* to have frame rate independence. The *y* component is not really needed here unless we want to use it to climb the hills at the edge of the terrain, overcoming the slope limitations imposed by the existing, and still active, *Character Controller*. The position of the character is then updated accordingly.

To shoot our pellet projectiles, we simply need to update the existing *bullet* script where, to ensure that the firing event is also triggered by the sliding magnet or button present on the Cardboard, we should add an additional check by using the *Cardboard.SDK.Triggered* flag as shown here:

```
using UnityEngine;
using System.Collections;

public class ShootingScript : MonoBehaviour {

  public GameObject bullet;

  void Update () {
    if (Input.GetButtonDown("Fire1") || Cardboard.
SDK.Triggered) {
    // create a new bullet in the scene at this very
location
    Instantiate(bullet, this.transform.
position, this.transform.rotation);
    }
  }
}
```

Anyway, automatic moving may not be the best solution in a different game, so we should also see how we can modify the script to move only when the magnet/button is held down. To make the script more general, we should also take into account the possibility that there is a gamepad connected and see how we could handle its input as well.

In this case, at the beginning of the *Update()* method, we need to call a new method, *GetDirection()*, to retrieve the player's input. Since we want to be able to also use a gamepad, our input needs to be stored as a *Vector2* to take into account the gamepad *x* and *y* axes.

GetDirection() starts by declaring two float variables, *x* and *y*, that will ultimately make up the vector to be returned. In case, on the one hand, the player is pulling the Cardboard trigger/button (or the mouse left click button when testing on PC), we can simply set *y* to 1 to signify forward movement. If, on the other hand, we have the gamepad, we need to actually retrieve the values from the predefined axis defined in the Project Settings/Input preferences. Once we have these, we can compose the vector to be returned.

Back in Update(), the method is essentially the same as in the previous case, with the notable difference that now we need to check for any *x* and *y* movement. This can be done simply by checking whether the absolute value of either one among the returned *x* and *y* components is greater than 0, something that can be achieved by using the handy *Mathf.Epsilon* predefined value. This is a constant referring to the smallest float number greater than 0 that can be measured by the system.

The script is as follows:

```
using UnityEngine;
using System.Collections;

public class VRmovement : MonoBehaviour {

  public float thrust = 1f;
  public Camera cam;

  void Update()
  {
    Vector2 direction = GetDirection ();
    // define a vector pointing up

    if ((Mathf.Abs (direction.x) > Mathf.Epsilon ||
 Mathf.Abs (direction.y) > Mathf.Epsilon)) {
      // move in the direction the camera is facing
      Vector3 moveTowards = cam.transform.
forward * direction.y + cam.transform.right *
 direction.x;
      // project vector on xz plane
      moveTowards = Vector3.
ProjectOnPlane (moveTowards, Vector3.up);

      moveTowards.x = moveTowards.x *
thrust * Time.deltaTime;
      moveTowards.z = moveTowards.z * thrust * Time.
deltaTime;
      moveTowards.y = moveTowards.y * thrust * Time.
deltaTime;
```

```
        transform.position += moveTowards;
    }
}

private Vector2 GetDirection ()
{
    float x,y;
    if (Input.GetMouseButton(0) || Cardboard.SDK.
Triggered){
        x = 0f;
        y = 1f;
    } else { // gamepad inputs
        x = Input.GetAxis("Horizontal");
        y = Input.GetAxis("Vertical");
    }
    Vector2 direction = new Vector2(x,y);
    return direction;
    }
}
```

In this way, though, we are using the trigger for movement, meaning that we won't be able to shoot at will like in the previous example. How can we try to accommodate both needs?

A possible approach would be to add a sort of "baby walker" ring around the Player prefab and in front of the main camera so that we can use the player's gaze to trigger movement, leaving the Cardboard button free to operate the gun.

To do this, let's add a new 3D object, a cylinder for example, as a child to FPSController and reduce it to a disk as shown in Figure 13.2. We can call it "walker" and place it exactly at the center of FPSController. Now change its *y* component to make it negative (−0.3 or −0.4 relative to the camera should be enough), so it will be visible in the lower part of the screen when playing, and remove its original capsule collider to add a *Mesh Collider* instead. The latter will base the collider on the actual mesh of the object. Last, we should also add an "Event Trigger" component where we define two events, **Pointer Enter** and **Pointer Exit**, to track the player's gaze (Figure 13.3).

The object to reference in *Event Trigger* is "walker" itself, while a new, small script is needed. We can call it "CamFollow," and all it has to do is retrieve the *VRMovement* script in the parent and call a new method

FIGURE 13.2   A disk working as a "baby walker" for FPSController: just looking at the "walker" will make the player move in the direction that he or she is currently facing.

there, setting a flag used to start/stop movement accordingly. The script is like the following:

```
using UnityEngine;
using System.Collections;

public class CamFollow : MonoBehaviour {

  public void Clicked(bool flag)
  {
    GetComponentInParent<VRmovement>().Move(flag);
  }
}
```

VRMovement needs to be slightly reworked, as follows, to include a new Boolean flag, **run**, besides the *Move* method we are calling from *CamFollow*.

```
  public float thrust = 1f;
  public Camera cam;
  private bool run;

  void Start() {
```

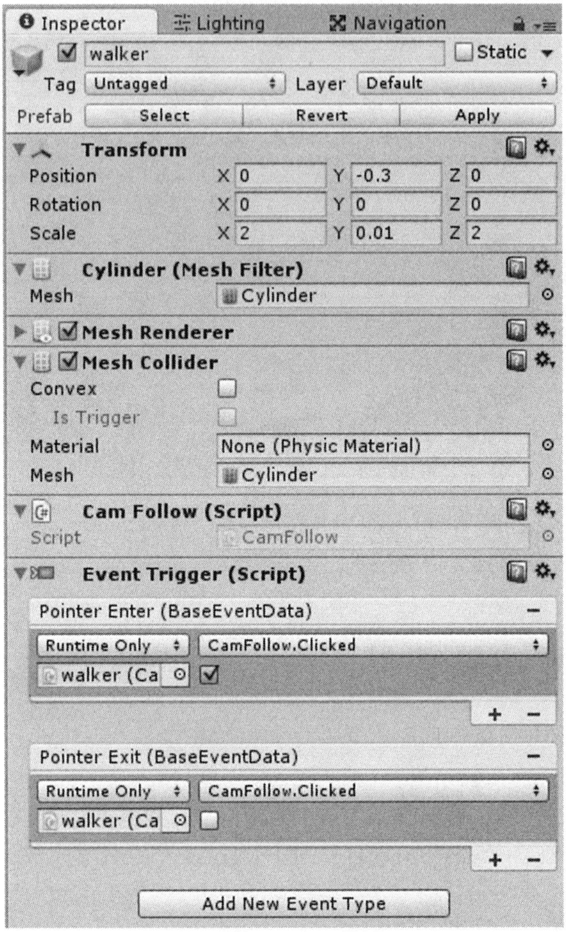

FIGURE 13.3   The different components of the "walker" object.

```
   run = false;
}

public void Move (bool flag) {
  if (flag)
     run = true;
   else
     run = false;
}

// move by "pushing" the walker, based on "run"
flag.
```

```
void Update() {
  // move in the direction the camera is facing
  Vector3 moveForward = cam.transform.forward;

  if (run) {
    // project vector on xz plane
    moveForward = Vector3.
ProjectOnPlane (moveForward, Vector3.up);

    moveForward.x = moveForward.x *
thrust * Time.deltaTime;
    moveForward.z = moveForward.z * thrust * Time.
deltaTime;

    transform.position += moveForward;
    }
  }
```

Last, but not least, to ensure that the gaze is properly implemented, don't forget to add a *Physics Raycaster* component to the main camera (make sure that its event mask includes the layer that the objects you want to hit are on!) as well as a general *Event System*, if you don't have one in the scene already. The latter should include a **Gaze Input Module** and a **Touch Input Module** instead of its default **Standard Input**.

We have now seen three different methods that we can use to implement movement in Cardboard-based VR games,* starting from one of the original Controller prefabs included in Unity's Standard Assets.

As a last exercise to consolidate what we've learned so far, we also need to familiarize ourselves with menu navigation in VR. We saw how it works in Chapter 12 within the Cardboard demo, so let's try now to make our own menu system with two items: one for starting the game (i.e., loading the Game scene we just did) and another to switch VR mode on and off.

Add a new empty scene to your project. Remove the default main camera, add a *Cardboard Main* object from the prefab instead, and then also add a *Cardboard Reticle* as an additional child of the new main camera.† Add a Physics Raycaster component to the main camera as well, to enable interactivity with objects by gazing at them.

---

* The VR Movement examples discussed here are implemented in the corresponding unity package available for download.

† If you don't see anything when starting the scene, be sure that the camera's Clear Flags is set to "Skybox" in the Inspector.

With the Cardboard controller set up, we can now focus on the menus. Add a new button from the **Game Object/UI** menu, retype its text to something like "Toggle VR Mode," and change its highlighted color to something like a bright yellow. As we know, adding the first user interface (UI) element will add not only the element itself but also a *canvas* and an Event System to the scene. Before proceeding any further, we should take care of setting these up properly. First of all, the canvas. Select the VR main camera to be its **Event Camera**, and change the Canvas Render mode to **World Space** so that any UI element will actually be a part of the scene and not a static overlay on top of it. We now have to move the button around so that it can actually be within the camera initial view. It's also a good time to repeat the earlier steps and add the second button with a text like "Start Game." In the end, you should have something similar to Figure 13.4.

Once this is done, we can add the *Gaze Input* and *Touch Input* modules to the Event System while removing the default *Standalone Input Module* instead. At this stage, we can already highlight the buttons when aiming

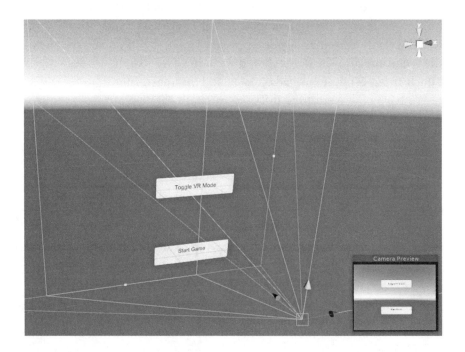

FIGURE 13.4 Setting up a UI for VR. The canvas is set to work in "world" and not "screen" space so that we can actually interact with the UI elements by pointing at them with the Cardboard Reticle.

at them by using the reticle as shown in Figure 13.5; however, nothing will happen yet by clicking, touching, or using the Cardboard button, as we need to code that functionality ourselves.

To do this, we simply need to add an empty object with an attached script—we can call both of them **VRMenu**—and then write the following,

```
using UnityEngine;
using System.Collections;
using UnityEngine.SceneManagement;

public class VRMenu : MonoBehaviour {

  public void ToggleVRMode() {
    Cardboard.SDK.VRModeEnabled = !Cardboard.SDK.
VRModeEnabled;
  }

  public void LoadScene(int i) {
    SceneManager.LoadScene(i);
  }
}
```

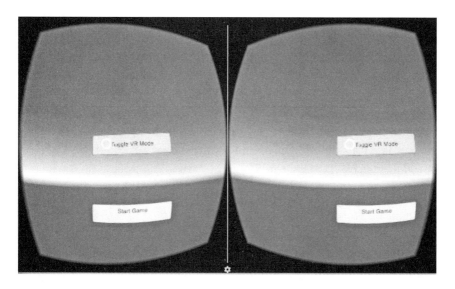

FIGURE 13.5   Adding the Gaze input module to the Event System allows us to trigger the button highlight state simply by looking at them.

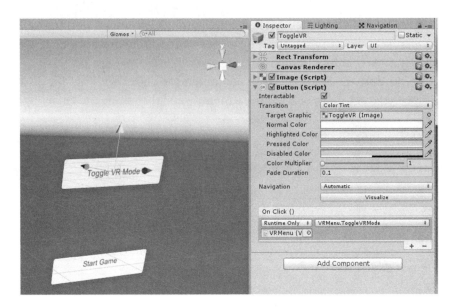

FIGURE 13.6   Setting up the Toggle VR button event so that it calls the ToggleVRMode() method when clicked. The same thing has to be done for the Start Game or any other button we add to the canvas.

where *ToggleVRMode()* simply switches the VR-enabled flag in the Cardboard SDK, while *LoadScene()* uses the SceneManager class to load a scene with the specified index. The two methods have to be called by properly setting up the *OnClick()* event in the corresponding UI buttons, as shown in Figure 13.6.

We now have a rudimentary menu system that we can use as a starting point to code a Splash screen for a VR game. If we wanted to also add a Quit functionality, we could simply extend the script by adding a similar method for a dedicated button to quit the application, or we could also automatically check whether the "Back Button" has been pressed via the appropriate Cardboard SDK method. In this case, we could use *Update()* or *LateUpdate()** like in the following short code snippet:

```
void LateUpdate() {
 Cardboard.SDK.UpdateState();
 if (Cardboard.SDK.BackButtonPressed) {
  Application.Quit();
 }
```

---

* A variant of the Update method that is called every frame after the latter has been processed. Useful to order script execution.

Congratulations! You now have the foundational knowledge needed to develop a variety of game concepts, from simple 2D and puzzle games to VR experiences! Keep up the good work and stay curious!

IV

Advanced Topics

CHAPTER 14

Physics

MASTERING SOMETHING MEANS UNDERSTANDING how it works, inside out. However, modern game engines like Unity allow us to use very complex technology apparently without the need to understand the inherent details. That may be true as long as we are satisfied with only a basic use of such technology, but the ability to know why things work in a certain way does give us the power to delve deeper into the underlying systems and, eventually, modify them to suit our specific needs.

3D games that want to simulate any aspect of reality have necessarily to simulate the physical world we live in, together with its laws, and for this reason, any game developer ought to have at least a basic grasp of math, geometry, and physics. That's why, in this chapter, we are going to discuss Newtonian physics and see how we can implement a simple Physics engine to recreate proper rigid body behaviors within Unity itself.

In his *Philosophiae Naturalis Principia Mathematica*, published in 1687, Sir Isaac Newton (1643–1727) laid down the foundation for classical mechanics by formulating the laws of motion and universal gravitation, enabling all of us, game developers living more than 300 years later included, to correctly model trajectories and interactions between bodies.

In particular, Newton formulated three laws of motion, which we will discuss now and play with within Unity.

NEWTON'S FIRST LAW

Newton's first law states that "*When viewed in an inertial reference frame, an object either remains at rest or continues to move at a constant* velocity, *unless acted upon by an unbalanced external* force." In other words, if we consider a body upon which no net force is acting, this body will remain at rest if it is currently at rest while, if it is moving with a constant velocity, it will continue to do so.

Before proceeding any further, we should also be very clear about how to combine velocities and forces, something that we have let Unity's built-in game engine do for us throughout the book so far. Remember, these are just vectors that can be represented in terms of their magnitude and direction, which are easily obtainable by considering their individual components.

See Figure 14.1 for a 2D example.

When adding vectors, the resulting vector is given by the sum of the individual vectors' components. Remember, also, that multiplying a vector by a scalar means multiplying each component by the scalar value.

Let's now make a simple 3D scene in Unity where we can play around with forces. Start a new Unity Project 3D and add a sphere. If we run the scene, nothing happens. The sphere is still and remains still, in an empty world. Indeed, by default we are in an inertial reference frame, and we can start experimenting with velocities and Newton's first law.

Add a new script to the sphere (we can call it *PhysicsEngine*, for example) and add a private variable of type Vector3. Call it *velocity* and initialize it in the *Start()* function with something like

```
velocity = new Vector3(1f, 1f, 0);
```

This represents the original velocity that the sphere has when we begin our observation.

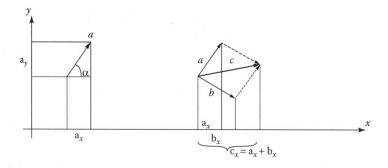

FIGURE 14.1   A vector *a* can be described in terms of its components (a_x, a_y). Its magnitude is easily computed by using Pythagoras's theorem. If, instead, magnitude A and angle α of a vector *a* are known, the components are simply $a_x = A \cos\alpha$ and $a_y = A \sin\alpha$.

We can delete *Update()* for now and instead add the *FixedUpdate()* function. Everything we do will be governed by the Physics engine, so this is the right place to update stuff. Here, we can simply add a line of code that will update the sphere's position, given its current position and the velocity:

```
this.transform.position += velocity * Time.deltaTime;
```

Remember, velocity is measured in distance units per second, so we need to multiply for *Time.deltaTime* to get the distance that the sphere traveled in between frames. Since we are in *FixedUpdate*, we actually know this function will be called at regular intervals of 0.02 seconds.

Back in Unity, run the scene: in accordance with the law of inertia, the sphere will continue to move with its initial velocity.

Anyway, what Newton's first law really says is that the sum of external forces must be zero for the body to remain still or keep moving at a constant velocity, so we should extend our script to include external forces and check that the overall sum of these nets zero.

To do so, let's first add the following line to the beginning of the script:

```
using System.Collections.Generic;
```

This allows us to use lists, which will come in handy here to handle different forces. Indeed, right after the definition of velocity in the script, we can now define, besides a Vector3 *netForce*, a list of *forces*:

```
public Vector3 netForce;
public List<Vector3> forces = new List<Vector3>();
```

What we want our script to do now is check whether all the forces applied to the sphere cancel each other. If so, we can move the sphere according to its original velocity vector. If not, we should stop, since we are entering a situation not covered by Newton's first law.

Let's define a new method, *SumForces()*, where we add the external forces together. Here, we can reset netForces by using the *Vector3.zero* instruction and then use a *foreach* loop to go through all the vectors in our list of forces, adding each to netForce like this:

```
foreach (Vector3 forceVector in forces)
        {
            netForce += forceVector;
        }
```

Then, we can modify FixedUpdate() to include a call to SumForces(), so that every 0.02 seconds we check what is the value of netForce, and react accordingly: if netForce is zero, we update the sphere's position like we did earlier while, in case there are forces applied, we print and send a message to the console and do nothing, waiting for further instructions.

Overall, the script will now look like the following:

```
using UnityEngine;
using System.Collections;
// to have lists
using System.Collections.Generic;

public class PhysicsEngine : MonoBehaviour {

  // the original velocity of the sphere
  private Vector3 velocity;
  // tracking all the forces applied to the sphere
  public Vector3 netForce;
  public List<Vector3> forces = new List<Vector3>();
    // updated at constant intervals of 0.02s, i.e.
    50 times a second
  void FixedUpdate ()
  {
    SumForces();

    if (netForce == Vector3.zero)
    {
        this.transform.position += velocity * Time.
        deltaTime;
    }
    else
    {
        print("Unbalanced force!");
    }
     }

  void SumForces()
  {
    // we initialize the vector3
    netForce = Vector3.zero;
```

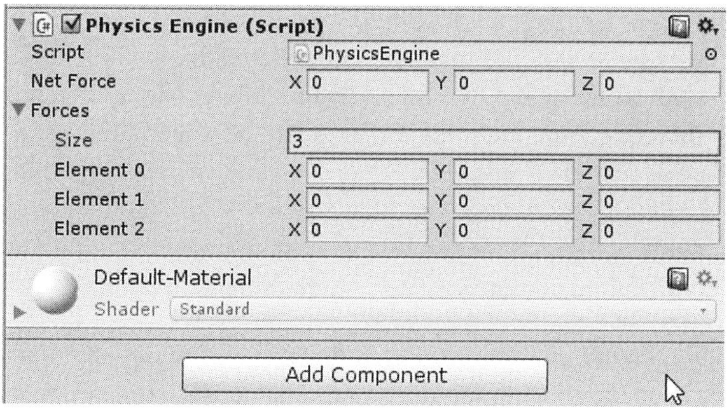

FIGURE 14.2   Adding forces.

```
foreach (Vector3 forceVector in forces)
{
    netForce += forceVector;
}
}
}
```

Back in the Editor, expand the Forces list to add two or three elements to the list (Figure 14.2), and run the scene. The sphere will start moving with its initial velocity but, if we now add an external force, the script will make it stop and print a message on the Console window. The sphere will move again only if we cancel out the unbalancing force.

We are now ready to introduce Newton's second law.

NEWTON'S SECOND LAW

"The vector sum of the forces F acting on an object is equal to the mass m of that object multiplied by the acceleration vector a of the object" or $F = m\,a$.

We can now update the PhysicsEngine script to properly handle forces.

Specifically, after adding a new public variable for the mass of our sphere,* we need to include also an *UpdateVelocity()* method, where we first compute the acceleration as *F/m* and then update the velocity

_____

* If we assume that Unity's distance unit is 1 meter, we can also assume that we are inputting the mass in kilograms. It doesn't really matter in a simple example like this whether we are measuring the mass in kilos, grams, pounds, or whatever, but always be sure that you keep your units consistent when developing an actual game! Remember, though, that forces are always a mass multiplied by a distance multiplied by time squared and are measured in Newtons.

accordingly. Remember, the acceleration is defined as the rate at which an object changes its velocity, that is, it is the derivative of the velocity with respect to time; hence, we can get an instantaneous change in velocity by taking the acceleration and multiplying it by Time.deltaTime.

UpdateVelocity() needs to be called after SumForces() in the FixedUpdate() method, after which we can just update the sphere position like we did previously. Note also that if no (or opposite) forces are applied, netForce will be zero, meaning that the resulting acceleration will be zero as well, and the velocity will not change.

The script should now be like the following:

```
public class PhysicsEngine : MonoBehaviour {

  // the original velocity of the sphere
  private Vector3 velocity;
  // tracking all the forces applied to the sphere
  public Vector3 netForce;
  public List<Vector3> forces = new List<Vector3>();

  // the mass of the sphere
  public float mass;

  void Start() {
    // the initial velocity for the sphere. It may be
    still, if you like.
    velocity = new Vector3(0.2f, 0.2f, 0f);
  }

  // updated at constant intervals of 0.02s, i.e. 50
  times a second
  void FixedUpdate() {
    // compute forces acting on the object and update
    velocity accordingly
    SumForces();
    UpdateVelocity();
    // last, update the position
    this.transform.position += velocity * Time.
    deltaTime;
  }

  void SumForces() {
```

```
    // we initialize the vector3
    netForce = Vector3.zero;

    // add applied forces a vector at a time
    foreach (Vector3 forceVector in forces)
    {
      netForce += forceVector;
    }
  }

  void UpdateVelocity() {
    // a = F / m
    Vector3 acceleration = netForce / mass;

    // remember a = dv / dt !
    velocity += acceleration * Time.deltaTime;
  }
}
```

Don't forget to specify a number for the sphere's mass in the Inspector and run the scene, where you can now freely experiment by applying different forces on the sphere and see how its movement and trajectory change in a 3D space.

Simulating Gravity

It is now a good moment to simulate gravity by defining a new method like the following. This should be called in *Start()* so that later, in *FixedUpadte()*, it will eventually be added to any other external force that we may add from the Inspector:

```
void AddGravity()  {

  // gravity acceleration, along the y axis in
  negative direction
  Vector3 g = new Vector3(0f, -0.98f, 0f);
  // gravity force
  Vector3 gForce = g * mass;
  // add the gravity force to the list
  forces.Add(gForce);
}
```

NEWTON'S THIRD LAW

"When one body exerts a force on a second body, the second body simultaneously exerts a force equal in magnitude and opposite in direction on the first body."

Newton's third law is also called the law of "action and reaction," since it states that, for every action force, there is always a reaction equal in magnitude and opposite in direction. For example, if two ice skaters stand next to each other like in Figure 14.3, and one pushes the other in one direction, the pusher will experience the same but opposite force pushing him or her as well.

The same thing happens when we are swimming: we push water backward which, in turn, pushes us forward. Or, imagine a situation where we are carrying a heavy object while standing on a skateboard: if we throw the object away, that is, we apply a force to it, it will also exert the same and opposite force on us, making us move in the opposite direction. This is actually the same principle upon which rocket propulsion works: rockets eject mass (fuel) with enough force to receive back a force strong enough to overcome gravity and be propelled forward.

FIGURE 14.3   Experimenting with Newton's third law on an ice rink.

We can actually try to simulate the thrust due to fuel combustion in our sphere, turning it into a sort of rocket, and to simulate the effect visually, we can start by adding a *Particle System* component to the sphere. As it is not our aim here to make particles look "good," we can leave most parameters at their default values except for a couple of things, as shown in Figure 14.4.

In particular, particles are by default emitted along the *z* axis. If you followed our example step by step, instead, gravity is acting along the *y* axis, and this is the direction that we want the particles to be emitted toward. To do this, we can set *Start Speed* to 0 and then check **Velocity Over Lifetime**, where we can specify a value, –3 for example, along the *y* axis. **Play on Awake** should also be unchecked, since we want the particles to be displayed only if the player activates the sphere's thrust, for example by pressing the *T* key.

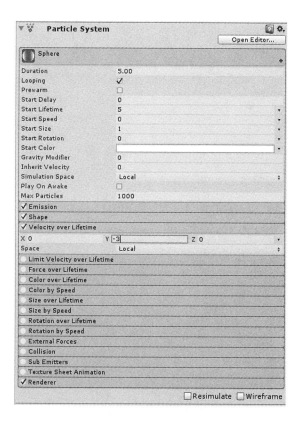

FIGURE 14.4   The Particle System component.

Moving into the script, the first thing we should do is add a few class variables to reference the particle system, to specify the mass of the fuel being burned and the desired acceleration resulting from the ejection of such mass.

```
// we simulate fuel emission via simple particles
private ParticleSystem fuel;
// the mass of the fuel we are burning
public float fuelmassBurning;
// the resulting acceleration due to fuel emission
public Vector3 fuelAcceleration;
```

In *Start()*, we add the reference to the Particle component,

```
// retrieve the particle component to access it later
fuel = this.GetComponent<ParticleSystem>();
```

and then, before anything else in FixedUpdate(), we should capture the player's input: when *T* is pressed we call an *AddThrust()* method, and when the key is released we call a *RemoveThrust()* method instead:

```
if (Input.GetKeyDown("t"))        {
    AddThrust();
  }

if (Input.GetKeyUp("t"))  {
    RemoveThrust();
  }
```

In the former, we take care of activating the particles, computing the force, and adding it to the Forces list,

```
// activate the particles and thrust forward!
void AddThrust() {
  // compute the force the Sphere receives back from
  fuel
  Vector3 fuelForce = fuelAcceleration *
  fuelmassBurning;
  // add force
  forces.Add(fuelForce);
  // play the particles
  fuel.Play();
}
```

while in RemoveThrust(), we stop the particles (also deleting any still on the screen via the Clear method), and we remove the thrust from the list of forces (to achieve this, we can keep track of how many forces have been added to the list thanks to the *Count* property and simply delete the last element, taking care not to remove gravity, which should always be present):

```
void RemoveThrust() {
  // removing the last added force
  if (forces.Count >= 2)
    forces.RemoveAt(forces.Count-1);

  fuel.Clear();
  fuel.Stop();
}
```

Last, remember that *fuelmassBurning* and *fuelAcceleration* need to be set via the Inspector in the *Editor*: play with the values to see what happens, and set them to slightly overcome the gravity force.

We now have a very simple demo simulating the effects of Newton's three fundamental laws!

To summarize, here is the whole script for reference:

```
using UnityEngine;
using System.Collections;
// to have lists
using System.Collections.Generic;

public class PhysicsEngine : MonoBehaviour {

  // the original velocity of the sphere
  private Vector3 velocity;
  // tracking all the forces applied to the sphere
  public Vector3 netForce;
  public List<Vector3> forces = new List<Vector3>();

  // the mass of the sphere
  public float mass;
  // we simulate fuel emission via simple particles
  private ParticleSystem fuel;
  // the mass of the fuel we are burning
  public float fuelBurning;
```

```
// the resulting acceleration due to fuel emission
public Vector3 fuelAcceleration;

void Start() {

  // retrieve the particle component to access it
  later
  fuel = this.GetComponent<ParticleSystem>();

  // the initial velocity for the sphere
  velocity = new Vector3(0f, 0f, 0f);

  // add gravity force.
  AddGravity();
}

// updated at constant intervals of 0.02s, i.e. 50
times a second
void FixedUpdate() {

  if (Input.GetKeyDown("t")) {
    AddThrust();
  }
  if (Input.GetKeyUp("t"))
  {
    RemoveThrust();
  }

  // compute forces acting on the object and update
  velocity accordingly
  SumForces();
  UpdateVelocity();
  // update position
  this.transform.position += velocity * Time.
  deltaTime;
}

void SumForces() {
  // we initialize the vector3
  netForce = Vector3.zero;
  // add applied forces a vector at a time
  foreach (Vector3 forceVector in forces)
```

```
    {
      netForce += forceVector;
    }
}

void UpdateVelocity() {
  // a = F / m
  Vector3 acceleration = netForce / mass;

  // remember a = dv / dt !
  velocity += acceleration * Time.deltaTime;
}

void AddGravity()  {

  // gravity acceleration
  Vector3 g = new Vector3(0f, -0.98f, 0f);
  // gravity force
  Vector3 gForce = g * mass;

  // add the gravity force to the list
  forces.Add(gForce);
}

// activate the particles and thrust forward!
void AddThrust() {
  // compute the force the Sphere receives back from
  fuel
  Vector3 fuelForce = fuelAcceleration *
  fuelBurning;
  // add force
  forces.Add(fuelForce);
  // play the particles
  fuel.Play();
}

// stop the particles and remove the thrust from the
list of forces
void RemoveThrust() {
// we remove the last added force, as long as we
more than two (the first is always gravity)
  if (forces.Count >= 2)
```

```
        forces.RemoveAt(forces.Count-1);
        fuel.Clear();
        fuel.Stop();
    }
}
```

EXERCISES

In our example, we did add a variable for the quantity of fuel being burned, but we are not actually simulating the engine behavior, as this would be way beyond the scope of this tutorial. We are only using it to compute the resulting force that the system has to apply to it via combustion to eject it and obtain the desired force in accordance with Newton's third law. Besides, fuel isn't unlimited, and we should also take into account a fuel tank level variable that gets decreased by the burning amount in every frame the thrust is active. Once fuel is used up, we shouldn't be able to thrust any longer. The fuel level variable should also be added to the total mass of the sphere for additional realism: as fuel is burned, the sphere itself actually becomes lighter, meaning that, with the same force, we can actually achieve greater acceleration.

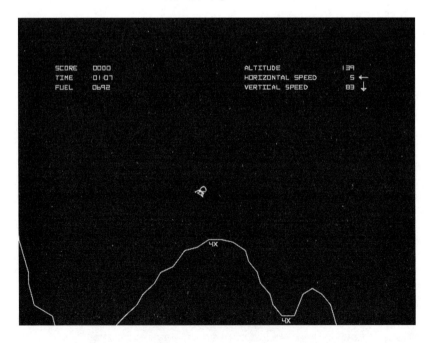

FIGURE 14.5   Lunar Lander (Atari, 1979): can you safely land on the marked spots by balancing gravity and the thrust of your engines?

Last, try adding controls for rotating the sphere, and have the thrust push accordingly:* if you can do this, you can proceed one step further and try making a simple clone of classical games like Lunar Lander (Figure 14.5), where you actually programmed all the physics involved without relying on Unity's built-in Physics engine! Congratulations!

* Be sure that the coordinate system in the *VelocityOverLifetime* component of the *Particle System* is set to *local* and not *world*.

CHAPTER 15

Introduction to Shaders

S HADERS ARE OFTEN ONE of the most mysterious and difficult components of game programming for beginners to grasp. Indeed, a proper
understanding of how they work requires some college-level math and
calculus skills, but we can surely try to appreciate their main features and
fundamentals even as beginning developers.

Every object in a Game scene can be represented in terms of **vertices**,
which are connected together to form basic shapes called *primitives* (like
triangles, for example). Each vertex includes information about its position, orientation, color, texture mapping, and so on and is then processed
throughout the graphics pipeline (see Figure 15.1) before being ultimately
rendered as pixels on a two-dimensional (2D) monitor screen.

In this context, shaders are short programs that help to project the
objects from a 3D space to a 2D image while manipulating colors and
textures accordingly on a per-vertex and per-fragment* basis to simulate
specific effects, like variable lighting conditions and surface reflections.

Shaders are usually written in graphic-specific languages such as Cg
(Nvidia), HLSL (DirectX), or GLSL (OpenGL), and Unity provides us with
different ways of writing shaders by using its own ShaderLab language,
which can also easily integrate Cg code.

Unity's shaders can be differentiated into three main groups: besides the
proper "vertex and fragment shaders" (VFS), in fact, we also have "fixed
function shaders" (FFS) and "surface shaders" (SS). These try to simplify

---

* Fragments are obtained by projecting primitive shapes between vertices in the 3D world into the
corresponding pixels of a 2D screen. They include position (x,y) and z-buffer depth, besides all
other information originally encoded in the vertices.

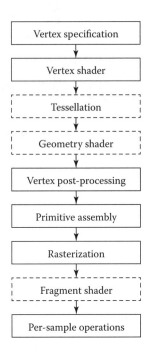

FIGURE 15.1 OpenGL rendering pipeline. The second, third, fourth, and eighth boxes from the top represent programmable stages involving shaders, while stages with dashed lines are optional. (Image taken from www.opengl.org/wiki/Rendering_Pipeline_Overview.)

the creation process by working at a higher level of abstraction and, in the case of FFS, it simplifies the definition of per-vertex lights in a way that maintains compatibility with older hardware. Here, we will have a look first at FFS, to introduce some fundamental concepts, and then at the more advanced VFS. Anyway, regardless of the type of shader we choose, all shaders in Unity share the same basic structure:

```
Shader"GroupName/ShaderName"
  {
    // properties that will be seen in the inspector
      Properties
        {
        }
    // define one or more subshader: the first
compatible one with the graphic card in use will be run
      SubShader
        {
```

```
// each subshader is made of one or more
"passes"
Pass
{
}
}
}
```

After specifying the group folder where the shader will be later accessed from, the shader is divided into two main sections: **Properties**, where we can define a set of variables that can be manipulated within Unity's Inspector window, and **SubShaders**. A shader, in fact, can have multiple subshaders to match different configurations and graphic cards: the first one found to be compatible with the hardware in use will be executed. Each subshader can then have multiple **passes**, which are executed in sequence to obtain the desired effect.

As a first, very basic example, let's try a **fixed function** shader to implement a simple rendition of the well-known Phong reflection model, step by step. As defined on Wikipedia,* the Phong reflection describes the way a surface reflects light as a combination of different components including a *diffuse reflection* from rough surfaces, a *specular reflection* from shiny surfaces, plus an *ambient* term to account for the small amount of light that is scattered across the entire scene (Figure 15.2).

To accomplish this, start a new scene in Unity and go through the following steps:

- Delete any directional light source in the scene, if present.
- Create a Sphere (*GameObject/3DObject/Sphere*).

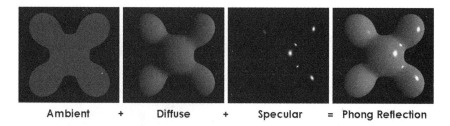

Ambient   +   Diffuse   +   Specular   =   Phong Reflection

FIGURE 15.2   The Phong reflection as the sum of its individual components. (Illustration © by Brad Smith.)

---

* See https://en.wikipedia.org/wiki/Phong_reflection_model for more information.

- Center and zoom in as you like.
- Open *Window/Lighting*. Remove the default skybox and set *ambient intensity* to zero. The sphere should now look completely black (Figure 15.3), since there are no lights now, but there is still a default material applied to it.
- Select the Sphere. In the Inspector, look for **Mesh Renderer/Materials**, and set Element 0 to none. The sphere is now "naked" and all pink to signify that there are neither shaders nor textures applied to it.
- We can now proceed in designing the various components. Create a new *Material* and name it **Phong**: this material will be dedicated to a shader simulating Phong reflection, starting from the ambient component of the light. Don't worry about the other fields in the Inspector: they are due to the shader used by default and are not our concern now.
- Proceed by creating a new *Unlit Shader* and name it "Phong" as well.
- Select the new shader and double click it, or right click and select **Open**.

By default, Unity creates a sample script for us (using Cg), but this is of no use to us now, so delete it. We are starting from scratch with something even more basic and, for clarity's sake, we will be adding the different components for simulating the reflection one by one.

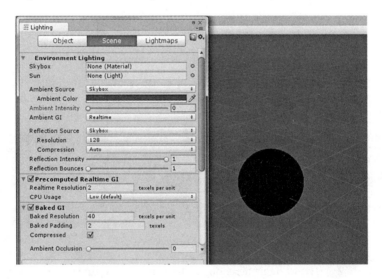

FIGURE 15.3   A sphere with no default light sources. The Lighting tab is accessible via the Window menu.

In particular, we are going to build a shader that, once finished, will implement the following components:

Ambient: The color the object has when it's hit by the ambient light set in the Lighting window (without this component, the ambient light defined in the scene would not be visible).

Diffuse: The object's base color when lit.

Specular: The color of the object's specular highlight.

Shininess: The sharpness of the highlight, between 0 and 1. At 0, we get a huge highlight that looks a lot like diffuse lighting; at 1, we get a tiny speck.

Emission (optional): The color of the object when it is not hit by any external light (think of this as a sort of fluorescent effect).

According to the reflection model, the full color of lights hitting the object will then be

```
Ambient + Light Color * Diffuse + Light Color
* Specular + Emission
```

We will also set the shader so that it can include a texture as well (this is actually required to show the specular effect, regardless of whether we want to apply a texture to an object or not).

Write this code to start the Phong shader, and include the Ambient and Diffuse parts:

```
Shader "ShaderTutorial/Phong" {
  Properties {
    _Color ("main color", Color) = (1,1,1,1)   // white
  }
  SubShader {
    Pass{
      Material{
                Ambient [_Color]
                Diffuse [_Color]
      }
      Lighting On
    }
  }
}
```

Here, the *Properties* block defines only a main color property and sets it to white with no transparency (RGB plus Alpha channel are all set to 1).

The syntax *_Color ("main color", Color)* identifies, first, the name of the variable to be used in the script (_Color in this case), then how it will be referenced back in the Inspector ("main color"), and finally, the variable type as defined in the shader language being used (Color). This is followed by an initialization value as appropriate.

The Properties block is followed by a *SubShader* including one *Pass*. This specifies one material where we assign the color property to the *Diffuse* function. Finally, we turn on the lighting processing. As we can see, it is all very straightforward.

Save and go back to Unity: by selecting the Phong Material, we can now access the shader we just programmed, as shown in Figure 15.4.

Once the Shader script has been associated to the material, notice how the Inspector allows us to modify the "**Main Color**" property that was previously defined in the Properties part of the script.

Drag and drop the Phong material on the sphere: the sphere is now black once again. Don't forget that we turned off all lights in the scene earlier, so we can't actually see anything yet!

Let's start by setting up a suitable *Ambient* light via the Lighting window in Unity. For instance, pick a white color and a low-value intensity,

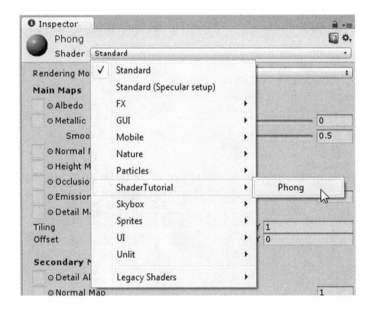

FIGURE 15.4   The shader we just wrote is now accessible through the Inspector.

for example, 0.60. The sphere will now look gray. We are now ready to see the full effect of our shader, implementing the diffuse component of the reflection model. To do so, proceed to add a *directional light* to the scene. Remember, position has no effect on directional lights, but their orientation does, so be sure to rotate it to better appreciate the effect of the shader (Figure 15.5)!

We can now proceed in defining the *Specular* part of the reflection. In the Properties section of the shader, add the following lines:

_SpecColor ("specular color", Color) = (1,1,1,1)
_Shininess ("shininess", Range (0.01, 1)) = 0.20

Here, we define not only the color of the reflection (white in this case, but feel free to experiment with other tints) but also a "shininess" value that, as the name implies, will make the surface of the object look more or less reflective (lower value = higher reflection). By defining it as a "range," we will be able to control it via a slider from the Inspector back in Unity.

In the Material block, we now need to add the following lines to call the predefined function with the values we just defined:

Shininess [_Shininess]
Specular [_SpecColor]

FIGURE 15.5　The most basic shader, providing a simple diffuse light effect.

And then, after the "Lighting on" command, we also need to issue the following command

SeparateSpecular On

This enables the use of a separate color for the specular highlight. Save the script, and the sphere back in the scene will look like in Figure 15.6.

We can now complete the shader by adding an Emission component and a texture.

Again, in the Properties part, add the following,

_Emission ("Emissive Color", Color) = (0,0,0.5,0)
_MainTex ("Base (RGB)", 2D) = "white" {}

while in the Pass code of the SubShader, we need to specify how the texture is going to be used, for example by adding

SetTexture [_MainTex] {
    Combine texture * primary, texture * primary
    }

FIGURE 15.6   Specular component added to the shader.

This instruction* takes the **_MainTex** defined in the Properties and processes each one of its pixels by multiplying it with the color resulting from all the previous operations (referenced here as *primary*). This is done both for the RGB value of the pixel and for its Alpha value (the multiplication part after the comma in the previous instruction).

In the end, if we select the sphere now, the Inspector will show the material with all the parameters we defined in the script, allowing us to change any value and add any texture. Note also how, contrary to what happens when we change public variables in a script at runtime, values changed in the shader properties will be saved and will not revert to the original ones once the game is stopped (Figure 15.7).

We may also end the shader with an additional line involving the command "Fallback." This identifies a standard shader to be used in case none

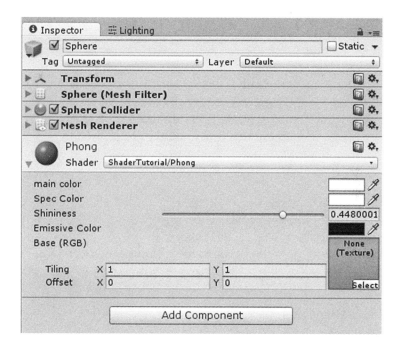

FIGURE 15.7   The Sphere object including the Phong material as one of its components. The material shows all the properties we defined in the shader script. We can now import any texture, and the reflection effect defined by the shader will be automatically applied to it.

---

* See http://docs.unity3d.com/Manual/SL-SetTexture.html for more information about SetTexture.

of the custom subshaders defined in the script turns out to be compatible with the specific hardware in use.

The final ShaderLab script should look like the following:

```
Shader "ShaderTutorial/Phong" {
    Properties {
        _Color ("main color", Color) = (1,1,1,1)
        // white
        _SpecColor ("Spec Color", Color) = (1,1,1,1)
        _Shininess ("Shininess", Range (0.01, 1)) =
        0.20
        _Emission ("Emissive Color", Color) =
        (0,0,0.5,0)
        _MainTex ("Base (RGB)", 2D) = "white" {}
    }

    SubShader {
        Pass{
        Material{
            Ambient[_Color]
            Diffuse[_Color]
            Shininess [_Shininess]
            Specular [_SpecColor]
            Emission [_Emission]
            }

        Lighting On
        SeparateSpecular On
        SetTexture [_MainTex] {
                Combine texture * primary,
                texture * primary
            }
          }
        }
    Fallback "Diffuse"
}
```

Now that we have a basic understanding of how FFS works and allows us to implement a reflection model, with or without textures applied to the object, we can proceed in exploring the more complex and flexible approach involving modern programmable hardware with an example based on Fragment and Vertex shaders.

VFS can be written in Cg within a Pass block in ShaderLab. To do so, we need to encapsulate such code with the keywords CGPROGRAM and ENDCG:

```
Pass {
  CGPROGRAM
  // compilation directives
  #pragma vertex vert
  #pragma fragment frag

  // the Cg code itself
  ENDCG
}
```

Notice how the first two lines of code are compilation directives: the #pragma statements tell the compiler there is going to be a vertex program (named "vert") as well as a fragment program (named "frag"). These directives are important, since using a custom vertex program will turn off all standard 3D transformation, while the fragment program will replace any texture combine modes defined in the *SetTexture* commands we saw in FFS, leaving us with complete control. Remember, in fact, that Vertex shaders are responsible for modifying the geometry of the scene and make the 3D projection, while Fragment shaders define the final color for each pixel representing the projected geometry.

Back in Unity, let's create a new object (e.g., a capsule), a material (call it "MyShader," or anything else), and a new unlit shader (which we may call "VFShader"). Open the shader, delete the default script, and write the following instead:

```
Shader "ShaderTutorial/VFShader" {
  SubShader {
    Pass {
      CGPROGRAM

      #pragma vertex vert
      #pragma fragment frag

      float4 vert(float4 v:POSITION) : SV_POSITION {
        return mul (UNITY_MATRIX_MVP, v);
      }
```

```
fixed4 frag() : SV_Target {
  return fixed4(1.0,1.0,0.0,1.0);
}


ENDCG
    }
  }
}
```

What do we have here? As we see, this shader has both a Vertex and a Fragment component. The **vert** function, which is always executed for each vertex making up the object that the material is associated with, simply takes in input the coordinates of the vertex (represented by a vector of four float numbers) and returns them* after multiplying the vector with the MVP matrix, that is, "Model-View-Projection," effectively taking care of the required transformations.[†]

The **frag** function, on the other hand, is even simpler and just decides that every pixel should be yellow (remember, color for each pixel is represented in terms of RGB plus Alpha components, i.e., another set of four numbers).

Very basic and very boring. To make things a little bit more exciting, we can try the following:

```
Shader "ShaderTutorial/VFShader" {
  SubShader {
    Pass {
      CGPROGRAM

      #pragma vertex vert
      #pragma fragment frag

      float4 vert(float4 v:POSITION) : SV_POSITION {
        return mul (UNITY_MATRIX_MVP, v);
      }
```

---

* Even though the output of the transformation will be the vertex position on the screen, that is, in a 2D space, four numbers are still needed here: two for the (x,y) values, one for identifying depth (z), and one for the homogeneous space (w). Homogeneous coordinates were introduced by August Ferdinand Moebius in 1827 and are widely used in computer graphics. See https://en.wikipedia.org/wiki/Homogeneous_coordinates for more information.

[†] The interested reader may check https://solarianprogrammer.com/2013/05/22/opengl-101-matrices-projection-view-model/ for a quick refresher in matrix algebra and to find out more about the MVP matrix.

```
fixed4 frag(float4 sp:VPOS) : SV_Target {
  return fixed4(sp.xy/_ScreenParams.xy,0.0,1.0);
                 }

  ENDCG
 }
 }
}
```

This time, the fragment part of the code receives the projected vertex position in input and returns the color of the corresponding fragment, where the Red and Green values are computed by dividing the (*x*,*y*) coordinates for the screen width and height (these are retrieved from _ **ScreenParams**, a float4 variable defined in "UnityShaderVariables. cginc" a file that is included automatically*).

A lot more can be done with shaders, and giving them some serious study can be great fun, besides being a very valuable skill from a professional perspective.

Additional sample scripts, showing how to draw a chessboard or Mandelbrot fractals for example, can be found at http://docs.unity3d.com/ Manual/SL-VertexFragmentShaderExamples.html.

---

* You will notice that many shaders scripts will explicitly include files like *UnityCG.cginc* to access a set of helpful predefined variables and functions.

CHAPTER 16

Setting up Unity Ads, IAPs, and Analytics

I N TODAY'S HIGHLY COMPETITIVE marketplaces, developing a good, or even great, game is only a tiny part of what developers have to do to be successful, and several other aspects have to be considered to have an actual chance of earning any amount of money.

Modern mobile games can follow several strategies to monetization, besides the standard "premium" model where players buy the game beforehand. These usually involve a combination of advertisement and in-app purchases (IAPs), and the latest versions of Unity do offer several options in this regard that can be accessed within the editor itself. Let's discuss advertisement networks first.

Ad-based games work by submitting targeted advertisements during the game or in between levels in a variety of formats, like banners, interstitial (full-screen ads), and so on. Usually, these don't affect the gameplay experience, and developers get paid either upon the ad being displayed or whenever players actually click on the ad and install the app being promoted. Recently, though, a new type of in-game advertisement has become very popular: the so-called rewarded ads. The idea behind rewarded ads is to actually use ads as a form of IAP to be activated only when the players themselves request them: the player himself or herself will willingly decide to watch an ad in exchange for some sort of benefit (coins, extra life, power-ups, etc.) in the game. This guarantees that players won't get annoyed by ads popping up at inappropriate times and lose interest in the game; on the contrary, they will watch the ads eagerly and keep playing as a result. Among the possible options available, several ad providers like Chartboost* and AdColony† also offer plug-ins for easy integration with Unity, but here we will focus on Unity's own network: Unity Ads.

Starting with Unity 5.2, it is possible to access an Ads configuration tab via the Window/Services menu. We need first to create a Project ID (Figure 16.1), after which we can start enabling ads and other features, like Analytics and IAPs, in the game (Figure 16.2).

Click on Ads and turn them on to start configuring their various options (Figure 16.3).

Once the age group has been decided, we will access a new tab allowing us to select supported platforms (e.g., Android and iOS), check a test

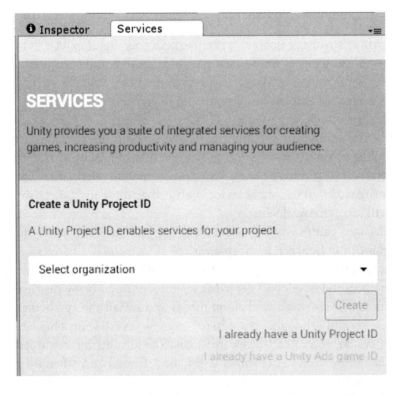

FIGURE 16.1   The Services tab. After creating a Project ID, we will have access to ads and other features.

---

* https://answers.chartboost.com/hc/en-us/articles/200780379.
† https://github.com/AdColony/AdColony-Unity-SDK/wiki.

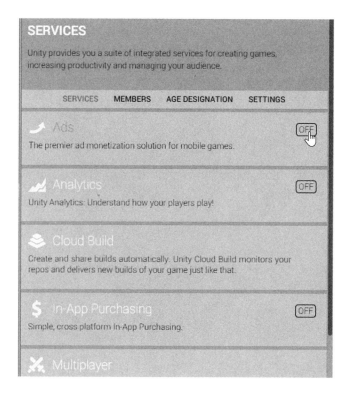

FIGURE 16.2   Once a Project ID has been created, we can turn on and configure any of the services provided by Unity.

mode that we should be using during development,* and get premade code snippets to integrate into our scenes for both simple and rewarded ads (Figures 16.4 and 16.5).

Essentially, the code needed for rewarded ads includes two methods: one triggering the actual ad display and another for notifying us of the outcome, that is, whether the ad was displayed in full or not, so that we can eventually deliver players with their well-deserved reward.

Where shall we insert that code? Rewarded ads should probably be triggered by a button press before the game starts or in the Game Over screen to get an extra life, while standard ads would likely be implemented in between levels or at the beginning of a newly loaded scene in its Start() method.

---

* Note that there is a limit to the amount of rewarded ads that can be displayed to a single user in a day (up to 25), but we can have unlimited ads for testing purposes. Naturally, testing ads, as well as ads showcased on testing devices, won't be monetized.

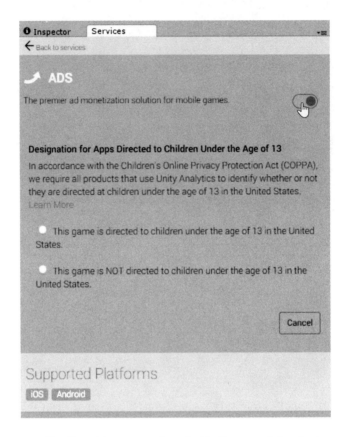

FIGURE 16.3   The first thing we need to decide for our ads is whether our game is specifically targeting children under the age of 13.

Anyway, once the code is added, we are not quite done yet, as we still need to sign up on https://unityads.unity3d.com/admin/. There, we can check our control panel where, for each registered project, we can finalize additional settings. Also, once the game goes live, we can link it to its corresponding builds released on Google Play or Apple's App Store.

Note that, to actually work, the string used to call an ad (i.e., *Advertisement. isReady(string)* and *Advertisement.Show(string, options)*) must match the one defined in the control panel dashboard, as shown in Figure 16.6.

Ads are easy to set up and are a very effective way of monetizing users who wouldn't directly pay for items in our games. Anyway, IAPs are still the main approach to making money in free-to-play games, and the new services integrated in Unity allow us to target different marketplaces, including not only Google Play and the iOS App Store but also the Windows and Mac stores.

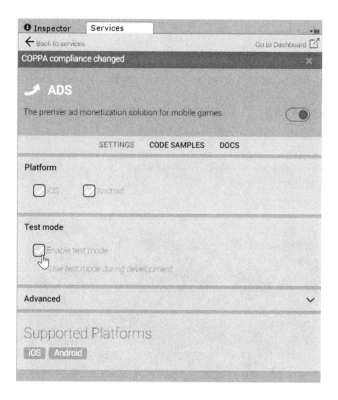

FIGURE 16.4   Remember to select Test mode during development. The specific game's IDs to actually activate ads on each platform have to be provided in the "Advanced" section.

With a Project ID assigned, we can proceed to also activate the IAPs from the Services tab. Note that, as shown in Figure 16.7, activating IAPs also activates Analytics (which will be discussed later).

Once enabled, Unity will ask us to import a new package with the required components that will have to be integrated into our game. The package will be imported into a **Plugin/UnityPurchasing** folder visible in the Project tab and will also include a demo scene for us to study and reference to check how things actually work (Figure 16.8).

The demo scene uses a script named **IAPDemo.cs**, which shows exactly how to implement all the various functionalities that we need to take care of in our own game.*

Essentially, Unity allows us to define three types of items that players can purchase: *Consumable* (e.g., virtual currency that can be spent

---

* Don't forget to add "using UnityEngine.Purchasing;" at the beginning of your IAP script!

FIGURE 16.5   Code snippets are ready to be copied and pasted for both simple (i.e., normal interstitial ads) and rewarded ads*.

FIGURE 16.6   The sample code may need to be modified so that the Integration ID specified in the dashboard matches the ad we call in the script (in this case, "rewardedVideo").

---

* The code can also be seen here: http://docs.unity3d.com/ScriptReference/Advertisements. Advertisement.Show.html.

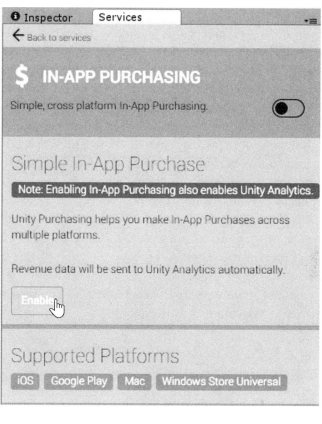

FIGURE 16.7   Enabling IAPs from the Services tab.

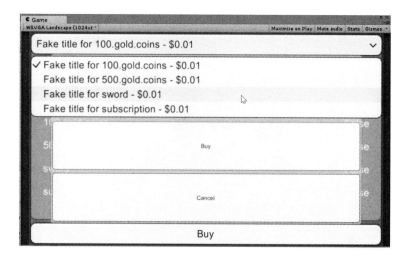

FIGURE 16.8   IAP demo scene provided by Unity.

in-game), *NonConsumable* (e.g., unlocking a new level), and *Subscription* (e.g., a purchase that will expire after a predetermined period of time and can be renewed). Each item needs to be uniquely identified, and the whole "virtual shop" has to be initialized, as shown in the script included in the corresponding page of the official documentation,* as well as in the sample script provided with the demo scene. The latter is the best overall reference and must be studied carefully, since all methods that we need to handle both successful and failed transactions, including special cases like deferred transactions,† are shown there. If needed, additional up-to-date reference material can also be found in the official documentation: http:// docs.unity3d.com/Manual/UnityIAP.html.

Last, but not least, analytics are an increasingly important aspect in the games business, since understanding players' behaviors is key to building an engaging experience and, without that, monetizing players effectively won't be possible.

Like ads and IAPs, analytics are also enabled via the Services tab (Figure 16.9) and cover all the common platforms.

FIGURE 16.9   Enabling Unity Analytics.

---

* http://docs.unity3d.com/Manual/UnityIAPInitialization.html.
† These are transactions requested by a minor who needs the approval of a parent/guardian and are a requirement specific to Apple's "Ask to Buy" functionality.

Once enabled, Unity actually allows us to test that the integration is working directly through the editor: simply press "play," and an "App Start" event will be sent to the Analytics service, updating the corresponding project on the dashboard. This is accessible from the link in the upper right corner of the Services tab and, once clicked, will open the Dashboard webpage for us. There, we can select a project and check all the relevant data.

The Analytics dashboard is made up of a few different sections:

- *Metric Monitor*, where we have a high-level view of the most fundamental data. Daily and monthly active users, sessions played, and so on are all displayed here (Figure 16.10).
- *Data Explorer*, where we can delve deeper into different metrics and compare them, checking also the game's performance across different time frames or geographical regions (Figure 16.11).
- *Funnel Analyzer*, where we can check how far players are getting into the game and where they stop playing (Figure 16.12).

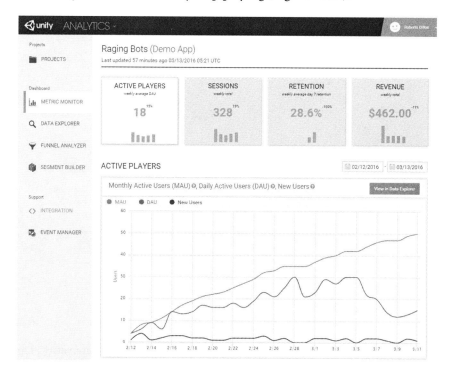

FIGURE 16.10   The dashboard for the Raging Bots Unity demo project showcasing Analytics' main features.

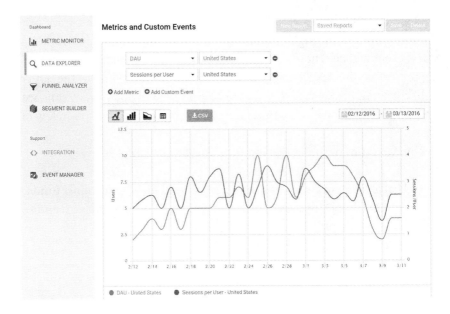

FIGURE 16.11   Comparing daily active users (DAU) with sessions per user in the United States for a demo project.

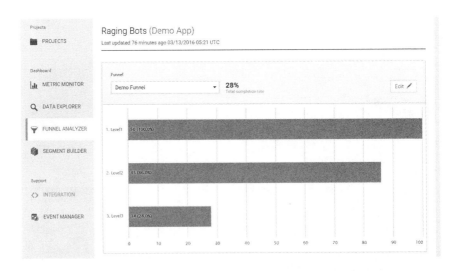

FIGURE 16.12   The Funnel Analyzer. This piece of information is often critical to spot possible issues (e.g., where the game may become too difficult and frustrate players) and fine-tune our games.

Name	Category	Description	Members
All Current Users	All Current Users	Composite profile of everyone who has used your app in the last 90 days. They reflect high level trends in traffic flowing to your app and generalized health over time.	50
1-3 Days	Life Cycle	Profile of users in their first 3 calendar days since joining the app. These are your newest users and present an opportune target for building long term user relationships.	3
4-7 Days	Life Cycle	Profile of users in their first 4-7 calendar days since joining the app. Strong engagement during this time period is often correlated with long term engagement within your app.	5
8-14 Days	Life Cycle	Profile of users in their first 8-14 calendar days since joining the app. Engagement should be continuously encouraged during this time using personalized messaging to keep users motivated.	9

FIGURE 16.13   In the Segment Builder section, we can fine-tune existing criteria to segment our players or create new ones.

- *Segment Builder*, where can check and fine-tune all the predefined segments used to break down and study our players (including sub-categories like Geography, Monetization, Demographics, etc.) or even create ad hoc ones matching our specific needs (Figure 16.13).

As usual, for up-to-date information, don't forget to check Unity's official analytics documentation: http://docs.unity3d.com/Manual/UnityAnalytics.html.

Index